THE WRITINGS OF BRENDAN BEHAN

PERSONA
GIVE T

Items should h

in the Library

Colbert Kearney

THE WRITINGS OF BRENDAN BEHAN

I have a kind of self resides with you;
But an unkind self, that itself will leave
To be another's fool. I would be gone.
Shakespeare, *Troilus and Cressida*

Gill and Macmillan

First published in Ireland in 1977

Gill and Macmillan Limited
15/17 Eden Quay
Dublin 1
and in London through
association with the
Macmillan Publishers Group

© Colbert Kearney 1977

Gill and Macmillan SBN 7171 0817 1

Extracts from Brendan Behan, *The Quare Fellow*, are reprinted by permission
of Methuen and Co.
Extracts from Brendan Behan, *An Giall*, are reprinted by permission of Mrs
Brendan Behan.
Extracts from Brendan Behan, *Borstal Boy*, are reprinted by permission of the
Hutchinson Publishing Group Ltd.
Brendan Behan's poems appear here in translations by Colbert Kearney. They
first appeared in the original Irish in the periodical *Comhar* who have given
permission for their appearance in translation, as also have Sáirséal agus Dill
who published 'Jackeen ag Caoineadh na Blascaod' and 'Guí an Rannaire' in

Printed in England by
Bristol Typesetting Co. Ltd Barton Manor St Philips Bristol

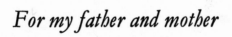

For my father and mother

Contents

ACKNOWLEDGMENTS

I should like to thank my wife Jean for encouragement and assistance throughout the writing of this book, Seamus de Burca who gave everything he had, knew or could find out, Seán Ó Briain who was generous with his recollections and his copy of *Lá Breá san Roilg*, Mrs Beatrice Behan who enabled me to read *the catacombs*. My thanks are also due to Professors Seán Ó Tuama, Seán Lucy and John A. Murphy, to Maitiú Ó Néill, Eamonn Corcoran, Sean O'Faolain, John Jordan, Christopher Logue, Michael McInerney, Tomás Mac Anna, John Ryan, Eoghan Ó hAnluain, Breandán Ó Buachalla, Sean Nolan, Johnny Devlin, the archives departments of *The People* and *Vogue*, the staffs of the National Library of Ireland, of the Morris Library of the University of Southern Illinois and, especially, of the library of University College Cork.

Preface

Flann O'Brien, writing immediately after Behan's death, described him as 'much more a player than a playwright', and claimed that any attempt to rank him with other writers would be mistaken.

> [Behan] was something better—a delightful rowdy, a wit, a man of action in many dangerous undertakings where he thought his duty lay, a reckless drinker, a fearsome denouncer of humbug and pretence, and sole proprietor of the biggest heart that has beaten in Ireland for the last forty years.

Many of those who knew Behan personally would agree that he was more than a writer, that his life contained more comedy and more tragedy than he managed to compress into his works, but, increasingly, his reputation will depend on those works—a novel, two plays, a handful of stories and poems. This book does not attempt to comprehend or resolve the Behan enigma, merely to survey and estimate his performance as a writer. It would be impossible to do this without referring to his life and his political affiliations but I have tried to keep such references to a minimum.

I

Tradition and the Individual Talent

Tradition

Brendan Behan was born in Dublin on 9 February 1923, during the Irish Civil War; at the time, his father, Stephen Behan, was confined as a republican prisoner in Kilmainham Jail. When he was eight years of age, Brendan joined the junior ranks of the IRA, beginning an involvement with Irish republicanism for which he later served two years' detention in England, 1939–1941, four years' imprisonment in Ireland, 1942–1946, and four months in England again in 1947. His literary career, which began during his early teens in republican magazines, was strongly influenced by his political experiences: *Borstal Boy* describes his first sentence in England, *The Quare Fellow* is an account of an execution which took place while he was imprisoned in Dublin's Mountjoy Jail, and *The Hostage* deals with an IRA kidnapping of a British soldier. Though many within the IRA believed that he brought the movement into disrepute during his latter years of fame and notoriety, he was nevertheless given a full military-style funeral by the IRA when he died in March 1964.

To say that Behan was born into a republican family, as if to imply that his later commitment to the IRA was inevitable, is misleading. On his release in 1923, Behan's father had abandoned his republican activities. It was not that he had come to support the Free State government or that he had lost sight of the ideals for which he had been imprisoned but, more of a realist than an idealist, he decided that with the defeat of the republicans in the Civil War and with his new responsibilities as a married man his duty was to support his family rather than to take any part in prolonging the national conflict. In 1922 he had married Kathleen Furlong, a young widow with two children, whose first husband, a Belfast man called Jack Furlong, had fought in the rising of

Easter 1916 and had died the following year of influenza. Kathleen's own family was staunchly republican. Her brother, Peadar Kearney, had been on the Supreme Council of the clandestine Irish Republican Brotherhood, had taken part in the Easter rising and had been interned during the subsequent War of Independence; her sister Maura was married to Mick Slater who had fought alongside her brother Peadar in 1916. If Stephen was inclined to adapt his aspirations to circumstances, Kathleen proceeded in defiance of them, brandishing her personal amalgam of extreme republicanism, socialism and Catholicism. While he was serious beneath a veneer of sarcastic iconoclasm, she burned with a rare intensity and tried to infuse her children with devotion to church and country.

Although Behan's biographer was right to point out that Brendan 'was not in the true sense of the word a slum-boy', it would be wrong to deduce that the family was other than what is meant by poor.[1] True, up to the death of Stephen's mother in 1935, the family lived rent-free, but neither this concession nor Stephen's skill as a painter was adequate security for a family at a time when few painters managed to find work throughout the winter. Both of Behan's parents had known middle-class comfort, but not during their married life. Stephen's father was a foreman house-painter who could afford to send his son to the Jesuit seminary at Knockbeg; on his death, Stephen's mother married another painter, Patrick English, and around this time Stephen left the seminary and became apprenticed to his step-father. His mother was a capable woman who acquired two houses, in one of which Stephen and Kathleen lived. She outlived her second husband, by whom she had a son, Patrick, and died in 1935, disappointing the Behans by leaving everything to Patrick. Within two years the Behan's rent-free accommodation was demolished and the family moved to a new suburban estate.

Kathleen Behan's ancestors were farmers in County Louth. Her grandfather, Peter Kearney, had no great affection for agriculture: he apprenticed his son John to the grocery trade in Dublin and followed him there on the death of his hardworking wife. He made no arrangements for the disposal of his holding, reserving his concentration for a farewell gesture: for a fee of ten pounds he contracted to sow a field for the landlord's agent, sowed it with chaff and headed for Dublin. His son John enjoyed considerable success and owned two shops at the time of his marriage in 1881. (Six children survived, Peadar being the first and Kathleen the fourth.) He was not, however, successful for long: in the early 1880s he could afford to give one shop to his manager, Laurence Bourke, but towards the end of the decade he began to change his address with ominous frequency and, when he died in 1897, had been reduced to working as an insurance agent. The reasons for his decline are not clear. From what is known of his character it does not seem likely that he lost his business through lack of commercial skill or because of personal extravagance. He was a man of fixed ideas, an extreme nationalist. He would not allow his son to be taught a verse entitled 'I am a happy little English child', nor would he permit him to read an edition of *Treasure Island* which had a Union Jack on the frontispiece. He loved to take his children on walks through the city, pointing out places of historical importance, especially those associated with the cause of separatism. Strangely enough, it seems he had a contract to supply provisions to the Curragh Military Camp; perhaps his political principles cost him this lucrative connection and, eventually, his business.[2]

Behan's parents might often muse on how close they had been to financial comfort but the fact remained that they were almost totally dependent on Stephen's wages. The exemption from rent was a great help but came to an end when Brendan, Stephen's eldest child, was only twelve. There were four younger children and two older stepsons to be provided for. The pride which differentiated the Behans from their neighbours was not economic; it was intellectual.

Stephen Behan was no ordinary painter and the mixed regard in which his mates held him was not entirely due to his skill as a sign-writer. Stephen's academic training placed him slightly apart from them: it showed in his range of interests, his confidence in himself and in his powers of expression and, most of all, in his detachment. He gave the impression that he was never totally engrossed in the life he was leading, that one part of him was withdrawn from it, observing it sardonically. His own youthful experiences made him slow to surrender to banners or slogans or to dedicate his life to the pursuit of security and wealth. He was not embittered, merely convinced of the comic facts of life. He did not fulminate against the enthusiasms of others: he chose wit rather than rant. He claimed that he had been expelled from the seminary because he had been discovered seducing a maid, a claim which many who knew Stephen's fondness for the tall tale were inclined to doubt. Ulick O'Connor suggests that Stephen lacked ambition and that he was disturbed by his mother's second marriage.[3] He may indeed have suffered a Hamlet-like crisis or perhaps financial difficulties, real or imagined, caused him to follow a trade, but the more likely explanation is that he was constitutionally unsuited to the priestly discipline and was sufficiently practical to leave the seminary. That he should advertise the expulsion and the attempted seduction is telling. The loss of vocation was not a topic for polite conversation, yet Stephen welcomed the double image of 'spoiled priest', the priest and the sinner, the sacred and profane; that it had the power to shock people by seeming to look lightly on two taboo areas, religion and sex, suited him down to the ground. He was seen as special, almost as if he had come back from another life, not altogether overawed by what he had learned. Yet those aspects of his personality which had attracted him to the seminary remained; he might mock priests and avoid churches but he never lost his faith in a divine comedian. The seminary left its mark, widening the scope of his mind and cultivating a delight in the subtle shades of thought and argument.

The limited independence achieved by the Free State led to his disenchantment. While those of his contemporaries who supported de Valera in the Civil War maintained that full independence would introduce a golden age, Stephen accepted the *de facto* Free State and turned to a more practical objective, the improvement of working-class conditions through the trade union movement. The seminary, the political prison and the cold winds that blow around the top of a painter's ladder moulded a wit that was able to make some saving sense of it all, sardonic, iconoclastic and hilarious. Take his version of the *Famine Song*, a slow ululation of the sufferings of the Irish as a result of the potato blight in the mid-nineteenth century, the first three lines delivered with grief.

Oh, the praties they were small over here,
Oh, the praties they were small over here,
Oh, the praties they were small, but we ate them skin and all,
They were better than fuck-all over here.[4]

Here is the laugh in the face of gloom, the coupling of traditional faith and the hard fact, which would become the trade-mark of his son's writing. Stephen's wry grin was essentially a protective device which he used to shield himself against the frustrations of the world. It did not always serve: throughout his life he was susceptible to violent bursts of temper, but these were soon forgotten or forgiven because the man's irresistible humour was more characteristic of him.

His wife's manner was always more flamboyant. She was possessed of a pure faith which simply pushed aside the mountains and the molehills on which he exercised his mind. Very much her father's child, she knew by heart the list of evils which England had inflicted on Ireland and she spoke of Ireland's heroes as if personally acquainted with them. Like her father before her, she took her children walking through the city, pointing out places associated with famous men. So great was her admiration for and her identification with all things which testified to the greatness of the race, especially in matters of politics and culture, that her neighbours sometimes mistook this pride for personal arrogance. Her self-possession arose out of a unique and at times paradoxical combination of republican and socialist principles with unquestioning devotion to the Church which proscribed them.[5]

She was forever singing. The history of Ireland—from the Irish point of view—has been for centuries transmitted in song and story. Earlier poets had enshrined in imaginative lyrics the plight of the oppressed people, lamenting the defeat of the native order and vilifying the invader. When in the nineteenth century Irish ceased to be 'the vernacular of the vast majority of the people, the native tradition was continued in English ballads. Kathleen's brother, Peadar, wrote some of the best patriotic ballads of his day and Kathleen shared the family fondness for songs. She would sometimes fit a tune to verses which pleased her but this was not to remedy a deficiency in her repertoire. What pious ejaculations are to the saint, patriotic songs were to her. In days of economic hardship and partial political freedom, she was never short of words or music to express her faith in Ireland and her hopes for England's downfall.

Music pervaded the Behan household, not all of it revolutionary. Stephen played light classical airs on the violin and sang songs which often contrasted with those of his wife. Two of his specialities were *Glendalough*, which tells how the hermit St Kevin terminated the attentions of a young female admirer, and *The Slide-Trombone*, in which with much *double entendre* the singer describes the virtuosity of his favourite instrument. The latter was accompanied by a wide range of physical contortion. He also had a talent for adapting material, but here again his productions were saltier than those of his wife. Kathleen sometimes demurred but young Brendan enjoyed them: 'But honest to Jesus, you'd have to laugh at my old fellow, and he put in bits like that into national songs, and it was all equal to him, he'd nearly put them into hymns, only he was never much where they'd be singing any.'[6] Stephen was a gifted entertainer, capable of enthralling children and adults with stories and musical interludes. He was also a remarkable teacher.

Undoubtedly, Stephen Behan was most content when ensconced in a snug bar analysing the ways of the world for his friends, but his income could not sustain this pleasure seven nights a week. When confined to his home he educated his children, not an easy task when the range of ages is taken into account. It was pointless to gain the attention of some if boredom led the others to interference: he had to appeal to them all at the same time. Nor was it sufficient to read or to tell: he had to make his material come alive, simple enough for the younger to follow, interesting enough for the older. He succeeded in casting a spell which his children never forgot, and showed himself to be a magician.

The curriculum of the little academy included Lever, Shaw, Yeats, Synge, O'Casey, Pepys, Dickens, Galsworthy, Zola, Maupassant and Dostoyevsky, as well as Boccaccio whom Kathleen thought a little too advanced and Marcus Aurelius who bored even the precocious Brendan. Here was the kind of education normally reserved for those with enough money to hire a private tutor. With his academic style and his knowledge of Latin and French, Stephen could command the respect of his class but was never tempted into magisterial dullness. To the younger he was a storyteller, to the older an ideal supervisor, witty, precise and memorable. For example, when Brendan read John Mitchel's reference to the people of Dublin as 'dastards', he assumed that Mitchel had originally used the more common 'bastards' but had been forced by literary etiquette to write 'dastards'. Stephen disagreed, pointing out that while one was born a bastard through no fault of one's own, one had to merit the title 'dastard'. Such lessons were not likely to be forgotten, and soon the boys acquired the father's love of books and argument. Brendan's step-brothers introduced their own taste which included contemporary authors, especially those sanctioned by left-wing critics. Home-life was dominated by words, the battle hymns of the mother and the comic songs of the father, the history of Ireland in story and print, political discussions of left and right, national and international. If the enthusiasm of the boys often clashed with the humorous pragmatism of the father, there is little doubt that he remained in the centre—however little they were disposed to admit it at times—and that he set them a standard of intelligence and style.

The essence of Stephen's talent was dramatic—the ability to know and control the emotions of his audience—and it is not surprising that they read many dramatists and particularly, among the novelists, Dickens. Stephen appeared in amateur pantomime and was also a regular attender at the Queen's Theatre. Kathleen's sister Margaret had married P. J. Bourke, an impresario who presented melodrama in the Queen's Theatre and who made the Behans welcome at his shows. As a very young child, Brendan was brought along and revelled in the atmosphere and in the glamorous illusions. The theatre was an extension of his father's ability to conjure up huge worlds of the imagination: the children relished the rich dazzle of pantomime, the agony and excitement of foreign parts in *East Lynne*, the drama of Ireland in Boucicault's *The Colleen Bawn* and—starring their own uncle P. J. —*Arrah-na-Pogue*. Emotional involvement was intense when P. J. Bourke presented what was probably his speciality, patriotic melodramas such as J. W. Whitbread's *Lord Edward Fitzgerald, Henry Joy McCracken, Wolfe Tone* and *Michael Dwyer*. Here young Brendan could see the heroic figures which were kept before him at home and sense the influence they exercised on the audience. He almost certainly saw his uncle P. J. raise hundreds to a frenzy of patriotic zeal with his rendering of Emmet's speech from the dock in the play by T. S. O'Maingean. He always remembered with great affection the genuine popularity of the Queen's Theatre.[7]

The Behans were distinguished by their intellectual and cultural awareness and by their study of words, but in their attitude to language they were far from unique. Dubliners of the day appreciated and cultivated verbal dexterity much more than they do now. They spoke a dialect of English which was enriched by elements borrowed from Irish, a relatively flexible syntactic structure which increased the possibilities of emphasis and variation, and a strong preference for concrete imagery which lent a certain crispness and immediacy to their expressions. While social classes were still rigidly segregated and before the advent of the mass media, local dialects tended to preserve their individual flavours and characteristics. In Brendan Behan's youth, phrases were admired, acquired and passed on. This tendency may be related to the cultural history of Ireland in which oral transmission played so large a part, engendering in the people an awareness of the past which sometimes strikes the foreigner as excessive. Behan was perhaps perplexed by the different rules which applied at school to English and Irish composition. In the Irish class he would have been encouraged to enrich his style by using *corraí cainte*, turns of phrase which have for some time been valued for their accuracy or colour; on the other hand, his English teacher told him to avoid phrases which have become hackneyed. The Irish classic is the English cliché. The retention of the *corraí cainte* may be a defence mechanism in a threatened language; English, secure, prefers originality. The people of the Behans' area spoke English but culturally they were in many ways closer to the native Irish tradition; their favourite turns of phrase were never reduced to the level of cliché. Of course, some words and phrases associated with the dialect were no better or worse than their equivalents in the speech of others, but a few examples will show how Dubliners could mould language into vibrant metaphors which combined imagination with the tang of actual life.

Your blood is worth bottling.
Changeable weather—you wouldn't know what to pawn.
He's a proper live-in-your-ear (-and-let-the-other-in-flats).

The use of such formulae is merely one aspect of an attitude towards language. In crowded living conditions, the ability to use the spoken word with skill and precision was the equivalent of a university degree in other circumstances. Among people almost all of whom left school at fourteen and who depended to a great extent on each other for their higher education and entertainment, the ability to tell a good story, sing a song well, was a passport to social success. To have a tongue like a hatchet was an important means of self-defence; to be able to coin nicknames which stuck was to limit the number of one's critics; to be able to turn one's arguments into satirical verse was to abolish them altogether. These people were acutely aware of their lack of formal education; of those among them who showed signs of outstanding intelligence they said that 'if they didn't go to school, they met the scholars'. Stephen Behan was one who impressed them but, typically, he was not content to illustrate the phrase. Not only had he gone to school and met the scholars but he had turned his back on them. Few could best him in argument or slanging match; he could hold his own, and more, in any company. When his young lad, Brendan, began to be noticed as a skilful user of words, they knew that 'it wasn't off the stones he licked it'.

The Individual Talent

Brendan Behan was a precocious child largely because of the education he received at home. When barely out of his infancy he knew by heart an enormous number of the songs and stories he had learned from his parents. He learned to read at an early age. Take, for example, Robert Emmet's speech from the dock in 1803. This fine piece of rhetoric was widely known, either from a volume entitled *Speeches from the Dock, or, Protests of Irish Patriotism*, or from framed copies of the speech which hung in many houses, including that of P. J. Bourke. The sentiments and the graceful delivery of the conclusion made it both a cardinal document of Irish republicanism and a standard party-piece:

> Let no man write my epitaph; for as no man who knows my motives dare now vindicate them, let not prejudice or ignorance asperse them. Let them and me rest in obscurity and peace; and my tomb remain uninscribed, and my memory in oblivion, until other times and other men can do justice to my character. When my country takes her place among the nations of the earth, *then* and *not till then*, let my epitaph be written. I have done.

More than a century later these words stirred men to hope that they would soon be able to write Emmet's epitaph. So moved was young Brendan that he learned the speech by heart. P. J. Bourke was amazed to find the seven-year-old reading his copy of the speech: having the sounds in his memory, the child could decipher the signs much more easily than other children. Shaw's *Preface to*

John Bull's Other Island was one of Stephen's favourite pieces and Brendan knew almost all of it. Where Emmet turned the force of classical rhetoric on England, Shaw used his impish humour and rare common sense, attacking the concept of the Anglo-Irish as anything other than a class distinction—much to the approval of the Behans. Such pieces were valued not only for aesthetic reasons; they were gospels of separatism to which the faithful could refer in dispute.

The same may be said of the songs which the child learned. The education he received at home lacked the disinterestedness which is the basis of liberal education. He was given a history of struggle and shown the ideal to which the struggle was directed, the freedom of Ireland. There was besides a good deal of laughter, but most children tend to be more attracted to idealism than to humour.

Neither conceit nor eccentricity was tolerated in the crowded rough-and-tumble environment of Behan's childhood, yet he managed to impress both his friends and adult acquaintances. To his friends he seemed older than he was, more articulate and tending to dominate, teaching them ballads, writing letters in verse. He sometimes revealed a desire to be famous, to achieve a fame which would bring people from all over the world to his funeral.[8] Meanwhile he often preferred the company of people older than himself.

The fact that his mother married twice provided him with two remarkable grandmothers who towered over his childhood like figures of tragedy and comedy and between whom he was divided as between a Scylla and Charybdis. His Granny English, Stephen's mother, was an exotic. She was a handsome woman, landlady of the house in which the Behans lived. Having survived two husbands she was fond of her own opinion and scorned standard theories of hygiene, exercise and diet. Enthroned in bed, her son and heir, Patrick, frequently beside her, she conducted her business, accepting the rent or the reason for its delay from her tenants and keeping herself minutely informed of everything which happened in her domain. She was a benevolent and convivial despot who always provided a jug of porter and a selection of dainty morsels during her levées. Until her death when he was twelve, Brendan was favourite, page and protégé; she plied him with alcohol and expensive food in order to ensure his good looks and his immunity from worms. He alone had entrée whenever he wished and he alone celebrated with her their victories over the forces of moral and physical enlightenment. In her court he experienced a world of hilarious hedonism very different from that he knew at home, free from economic restraint, spiritual commitment and radical ardour. With his Granny English and her cronies there was no fanaticism or idealism other than in pursuit of a good time and lively company; even her name, English, seemed to mock the patriotism of the rest of his family. Most of the women whom he met while with his Granny, whether in her apartment or on her progresses through the city, would not have been unduly enthusiastic at the struggle for Irish freedom; they probably knew more about Spion Kop and the Somme than they did about Aughrim or Benburb. They had close relatives who fought and died in the British Army and they had fond memories of the *ring-money*, the separation allowance sent to the dependants of serving soldiers. What young boy, tipsy with alcohol and rich cake, his head reeling with the colourful language and esoteric lore, could resist them?

With his innate interest in character and language he was attracted to a culture which was in many ways different from that he found at home.

On Wednesdays and I a child, there were great gatherings of British Army pensioners and pensionesses up on the corner of the North Circular, in Jimmy-the-Sports'.

When the singing got well under way, there'd be old fellows climbing up and down Spion Kop till further orders and other men getting fished out of the Battle of Jutland, and while one old fellow would be telling of how the Munsters kicked the football across the German lines at the Battle of the Somme, there'd be a keening of chorused mourners crying from under their black shawls over poor Jemser or poor Mickser that was lost at the Dardanelles. Jimmy-the-Sports' Bar did not at all relish the British Army or anything to do with it, but a publican is a kind above politics.[9]

And so was the young Brendan Behan when tempted by the songs and chat of a city which had been dominated for centuries by the British Army and which had evolved an ethos quite separate from that of rural Ireland.

Although Granny English died when he was twelve, she left her stamp on him. She had pampered and paraded him as a brilliant child: he performed at her command, basking in the praise and gifts which followed. She introduced him to a *demimonde* which would later provide him with valuable material and she fostered his talent as a performer. There was a price. Many feel that she spoiled him, giving him a taste for alcohol, luxury and limelight at a dangerously early age. Her favour fostered an unattractive selfishness in him which, when mixed with the short temper he had inherited from his father, led him to react viciously to any interference with his pleasure.[10] In fairness it should be added that her influence was not entirely detrimental: she was probably responsible to some extent for that strain of comic exuberance which informs his best work.

Granny Furlong was another matter. Fanatically anti-English, her home was open to those who shared her views. She sheltered those on the run and looked after their guns and ammunition. The Behans were regular visitors to her house on the nearby North Circular Road for musical evenings: Emily, her daughter, on piano, Stephen on violin, and the others singing. Here again Brendan was a favourite: his repertoire of revolutionary songs and his spirited delivery caused his Granny Furlong to see him as living proof that the younger generation would carry on the fight for Ireland's freedom. There is a very interesting account of a visit which he made to his Granny:

> One day, a little boy about eight years old, with coal-black curls, clear white skin and blue eyes, was ushered into the room and proceeded immediately to launch forth on Shaw, Yeats, Synge and O'Casey, in a most knowledgeable fashion for twenty minutes without stopping. When he finished, he became covered in confusion and rushed from the room, but not before those who had heard him had recognised that they had witnessed an unusual performance.[11]

The confusion is as noteworthy as the parade of knowledge. Throughout his life, friends of Behan detected a shyness which contrasted with his more usual bravado, but his bolting from Granny Furlong's house is perhaps indicative of something more than shyness. For as long as he could remember Behan had been able to impress people with his recitals of verse and prose. To begin with, it was merely a feat of memory, yet it was such as could earn him the applause he appreciated so much. He was, however, more than a memory-machine; he was also intelligent enough to realise—no matter how slowly—that there was a great deal of what he said that he did not comprehend. Perhaps on that visit to his Granny Furlong he glimpsed the unreality of his knowledge.

Apart from that, he must have become confused when he felt the contradictions and oppositions among the forces and personalities which were moulding him. The disparity between the worlds of his two grandmothers, between unselfish dedication to an ideal and selfish delight in physical pleasure, was only the most obvious. As he came to listen with some degree of discernment to the voices within his immediate family, he heard his mother echo the thoughts of Granny Furlong, his father and step-brothers proposing an international class warfare in place of old-fashioned republicanism, while none of them seemed to have much time for the comfortable escapism of the *oul' wans* whose company he enjoyed so much. His mother and his Granny Furlong had no difficulty in combining nationalism and internationalism with Catholicism. He himself was a devoutly religious child and would have heard clerical denunciations of all kinds of radicals; his father had no respect for the priests, probably because the Church had consistently opposed the fight for Irish freedom. Young children resolve such problems emotionally rather than intellectually— if they resolve them at all. He was swayed not so much by the arguments of his father as by the zeal of his mother. He longed to be great and she stood for a great cause : following her example and that of many who gained glory by fighting for Ireland he would give himself both to Ireland and to the Catholic Church. At the age of eight he transferred from convent school to the Christian Brothers and about the same time he joined the Fianna, the boys' brigade of the IRA.

His growing political awareness did not help him at his new school. The Brothers do not seem to have taken to him as the nuns did. When his mother visited the convent to express concern for her son's behaviour, she was told that she was rearing a genius. Later on, one of the Brothers came to Stephen and asked if he was helping Brendan with his exercises; clearly, Brendan's word had not been accepted. According to the story, Brendan had written an essay on 'French Influence on British Culture in the Renaissance' which struck his teacher as suspiciously good.[12] It is pointless to wonder how much a primary school student could know about such a topic; the important thing is that the story exists and indicates a lack of rapport between Behan and the school in which he received most of his formal education. Behan substantiated this in a letter to a left-wing newspaper, *The Irish Democrat*, some months after leaving: 'My teacher, for catechism instruction, used to read a chapter of Hogan's "Could Ireland become Communist?" For giving a very definite answer in the affirmative, I got a kick in the neck. Not from him, but from the lay teacher.'[13] The manner of the assault is curious but the essential conflict is clear enough. The Brothers set themselves the difficult but mundane task of turning out respectable law-abiding Catholic boys; they were not likely to be impressed by the flamboyant young rebel. Outside school-hours he was being taught to undermine the law they were teaching him to obey.

In many ways it was natural that, with his imagination, enthusiasm and background of left-wing republican protest, he should join the junior ranks of an IRA which was then socialist to an unprecedented extent. It was his opportunity to become involved in something bigger than his own area, to become part of that heroic chain of freedom-fighters whose images had always been before him. The Fianna were not like other scouts: the stress fell not on lighting fires or tying knots but on becoming mentally convinced of the need for the IRA and physically capable of joining it later on. Participation in the Fianna seemed to offer fulfilment to the two dominant elements of his character. He was, and would remain, a complex and apparently contradictory person: the shy stammering introvert and the ebullient extrovert, the weekly communicant and the spoiled brat, the universal charmer who would begrudge his brother a penny. As a member of the Fianna he pledged himself to the ideal of a free Ireland, offering his life to his superior officers to use it as they saw best; at the same time, through this act of unselfishness he put himself in line for action which might win him acclaim, even a place in history.

With his prior knowledge of republican history and theory he soon distinguished himself but he was not content to be prominent on an intellectual level only; he delighted in marches and demonstrations, especially if there was a risk of conflict with police or opposing factions, and by the time he was fourteen he was recognised as something of a veteran activist. On the whole, however, the IRA did not flourish during the thirties. Fianna Fáil under de Valera had come into power in 1932, with the help of the IRA, and de Valera had immediately set about rendering the IRA irrelevant. The Church, less subtle, continued to condemn the IRA, especially for its left-wing tendencies; this pressure led to right-left tension within the movement which became evident with the outbreak of the Spanish Civil War in 1936. Many left-wing IRA men left for Spain and Behan was only prevented from joining them by his mother who intercepted his correspondence. His application for full membership of the IRA was turned down because he was not yet sixteen. It was clear that the war in Spain was merely a prelude to a major European upheaval; traditionally, England's difficulty was Ireland's opportunity and the IRA decided to strike while England's attention was on the continent. In January 1939 they issued an ultimatum: Britain would quit Northern Ireland or face the consequences—an IRA campaign of bombing in England. Four days later the first explosions occurred. This was it—the resumption of the struggle; was Behan, because of his age, to be a boy scout while men risked their lives in England? It seemed so, until the IRA, perhaps sensing his restlessness, made him a courier. At last he was moving into the front line.

His first assignment took him to London shortly after Easter 1939 and the operation was successful if not slick. Back home he was soon ordered to the IRA training camp in Killiney Castle where he was instructed in bomb-making. His delight was obvious. Though he was the youngest in the camp he struck the others as older than he was and, despite the serious nature of the business, he was soon noted for his humour and his capacity to entertain with anecdotes in his highly individual dialect. Behind his easy manner was the thought that he was about to realise an ambition that he had had since infancy. Yet despite the fact that initially British security had been unable to cope with these early urban guerrilla tactics, the enthusiasm of the IRA did not last. Westminster showed no inclination to make concessions and the loss of civilian lives in England eroded any sympathy the English had with the IRA claims. On 25 August 1939, because of the panic of an IRA man, a bomb was left in a crowded part of Coventry, causing five deaths and many injuries; two IRA men, neither directly responsible, were later executed for this. By now, because of the activity of both British and Irish security forces—Dublin saw the IRA campaign in England as a threat to Irish neutrality— life became increasingly difficult for the IRA and by September the campaign began to lose impetus. Soon it became clear that it had been a failure and would be abandoned. Behan awaited instructions which never came.

Military discipline and common sense indicated that he should do nothing, but his enthusiastic imagination proved stronger. The prospect of another period of decline for the IRA struck him as both inevitable and unacceptable. His Granny Furlong had taken this view but she had done something about it. In the summer of 1939, at the age of seventy-seven, she had travelled to Birmingham with her daughters to conduct their own campaign; an explosion in the house where they were staying led to their arrest. She was sentenced to three years, her daughters to five and two. She showed traditional contempt for the court and, back in Ireland, received the traditional accolade. The *Wolfe Tone Weekly* for 26 July carried a poem by S. de Bhuitléir, entitled *Britannia*, 'inscribed to Mary Ann Furlong, sentenced to three years' imprisonment in England, July 14, 1939.'

> Britannia rules the nations,
> And Britannia rules the waves,
> Her rulers and her people
> Are the bravest of the brave.
> Her army is magnificent,
> Her navy without peer,
> She's mistress of the world
> Oh! she has nought to fear.
> Her greatness and her splendour
> No power on earth can shake—
> And—an Irish woman of eighty
> Makes the mighty Empire quake!

Granny Furlong's gesture underlined Brendan's inactivity but it also reminded him that those who struck against England did not always wait for explicit orders. He began to carry out private research on explosives in his own house, alarming his mother and angering his father who saw that the campaign was finished. By

November 1939 he could wait no longer: without official orders and despite the appeals of his friends he travelled to Liverpool. He showed great courage. He was sixteen years old, entering a country where even his accent would leave him open to hostility and suspicion. Detectives checked all arrivals from Ireland and even if he got past them he knew no contacts, no safe houses. Though he had been taught something about explosives, he had received no instruction in urban guerrilla tactics. It was an act of desperate courage and determination: he actually carried his bomb-making material with him. From a practical point of view it was stupid, doomed to failure, yet few had previously considered him stupid and many thought him highly intelligent. What prevented him from seeing that by going to England he was simply asking for a sentence in an alien jail where those associated with the IRA were normally subjected to special treatment? One cannot doubt that he intended to strike a blow for Ireland, that he saw his journey to England as an inevitable consequence of his upbringing and of his convictions. Yet others, equally committed, followed orders. In young Behan there was a burning desire to do something great coupled with a belief in his own ability to do it—a belief so strong that it swept all objections aside.

He was arrested in Liverpool and held in Walton Jail until his trial on 7 February 1940: feeling ran high against the IRA and he was made to suffer for it. At his trial he emulated his Granny Furlong, showing contempt for the proceedings except when they afforded him the opportunity to make a defiant speech from the dock. The Judge made it clear that he felt Behan deserved more than the three years' Borstal detention which, because Behan was sixteen, was all he could impose on him. Behan did not even serve three years: he found the life in Hollesley Bay Borstal Institution surprisingly congenial, behaved himself well and was deported to Ireland in March 1942.

Writing for the Cause

If I am anything at all, I am a man of letters . . . I have never seen myself as anything else, not even from the age of four when my mother says that when she sent me for a loaf of bread, I used to kick a piece of paper along the street in front of me so that I could read it.[14]

Thus Behan recollected in his last year when, aged forty, he was a very sick and troubled man. Though it is probably not totally accurate, it contains part of the truth. That he never saw himself as anything but a writer is contradicted by his association with the IRA: his invasion of England in 1939 was not in search of material even if it did provide him with the basis of a masterpiece. Yet his claim to have had literary ambitions at the age of four is credible and is supported by what is known of his childhood. The personality of the precocious child is best understood in terms of two apparently contradictory drives—a desire to dedicate himself to some noble ideal and an appetite for notice, approval and, ultimately, fame. It seems likely that even before he could read or write he delighted in imagining himself as one among those exceptional men who were cherished in his home—Pepys, Dickens, Zola, Shaw and the other writers whose works he heard read and admired. The idea of being a writer was especially attractive because it combined the notion of a lonely struggle in isolation with that of subsequent public acclaim.

Behan's childhood was dominated by two kinds of great men; those, like Dickens, whose imaginative creations would live and please forever, and those, such as the heroes of Ireland, whose unselfish devotion to liberty won the admiration and gratitude of succeeding generations. It could hardly have escaped the attention of Behan as he grew up that even in the case of patriots the fame which they achieved was preserved by words. In some instances, the degree of fame was due not to the political success of the hero but to the skill of the verbal artist. Many skirmishes had been transmuted into epics. Robert Emmet's rebellion had been brief and futile yet it would live forever. Emmet himself, a shadowy figure, seemed to possess little to recommend him to the ordinary folk of the city, yet in ballads he was to become 'bold Robert Emmet, the darling of Erin' and his relationship with Sarah Curran was to be seen as an Irish version of Romeo and Juliet. Historians might consider the fracas in Thomas Street as a significant gesture and little else but this would be wide of the mark: Emmet was a popular hero who epitomised the separatist dream of the Irish and kept their hopes alive through the dull routine of oppression. His apotheosis was almost entirely due to his speech before being sentenced to death; this endured as perhaps the most eloquent expression of the republican ideal and became a fixture in the hearts and homes of many Irish people.

If the idea of being a comic writer like Dickens was appealing, there was an even more attractive possibility. After all, Dickens was English and had not concerned himself with the cause of Irish freedom, but there were men who united pen and sword in the interests of Ireland. Wolfe Tone, the father of Irish republicanism who had committed suicide rather than be hanged by the British, wrote a fine autobiography in which he revealed himself as a likeable family man, an idealist with a sense of humour and a fondness for the bottle. Mitchel's *Jail Journal* was both a political broadside and a human story. Old Tom Clarke's *Glimpses of an Irish Felon's Prison Life*, for all its gentle style, was a spine-chilling account of the sufferings of political prisoners in English jails. Some of those who were executed with Clarke in 1916 were reputable writers, poets like Pearse and MacDonagh, and James Connolly the historian of Irish labour.

Literary ambitions were not surprising in a boy who had been brought up to revere writers and whose own verbal prowess had been noticed. Dublin had produced so many famous writers and his mother could point to the houses where they had lived—Swift, Sheridan, Wilde, Shaw. She had met Yeats and other figures of the Irish literary renaissance when she worked for Maud Gonne MacBride.[15] That these writers came from Protestant middle-class circumstances very different from his own was no deterrent to his dreams. What of two more recent Dubliners? Joyce—middle-class and lapsed Catholic—had made the literary world pay attention to the very streets and shops of Dublin, while O'Casey—working-class and lapsed Protestant—had re-created on the stage the tenements of Northside Dublin. Even nearer home was a man who, though his reputation could not compare with that of these great names, was probably a more powerful influence on Behan's desire to be a writer, his uncle Peadar.

Kathleen brought up her children to have an almost religious reverence for her brother Peadar; even at the height of his fame Brendan often described himself as nephew to the author of the Irish national anthem. As a child he saw Kearney as an example of what he himself longed to be: soldier, writer, socialist, celebrity. Kearney had fought in 1916 and had provided the rebels with their battle hymn, 'A Soldier's Song'. This was typical of neither his style nor his standard: Kearney was the author of some of the finest ballads of his time. He would hardly have called himself a socialist but there was an unromantic realism in his best work which rooted it in the ordinary life of the city. In 'Down by the Glenside' the balladeer encounters Ireland in the female form —a traditional device—but she is no longer a beautiful princess but an old woman whose poverty impels her to collect young nettles as food and who hums a song in praise of the Fenians who fought for Ireland in the nineteenth century. Two of his ballads commemorate the 1916 rising. 'A Row in the Town' describes the principal engagements with fervour and humour; 'The Three-Coloured Ribbon' is the song of a girl whose lover is killed in the fighting. More typical are 'Down by the Liffeyside', a spirited love song the strength of which lies in the combination of republican idealism and the social realities of city life, and 'Whack-fol-the-Diddle' in which the virtues of England and the vices of Ireland are catalogued with a fine irony. Young Brendan frequently visited Kearney and knew all his songs. Kearney's fame did not bring him financial comfort but this did not prevent Behan from seeing him as a 'National Poet', 'the city Raftery' who had consecrated his literary talent to the cause of Ireland's freedom and had earned a place in history.[16] It was encouraging for him to reflect that Kearney was no distant figure, removed by time or economic status, but his own uncle, a house-painter like his own father.

When the Fianna brought out their own magazine in 1935, he saw his chance to break into print. *Fianna: The Voice of Young Ireland* was the type of periodical to be expected from the junior wing of a military movement. Although it included some light-hearted material—short stories, jokes and competitions—it was essentially an anthology of republican propaganda, and practically everything it contained was coloured by its political objective, the education of republican revolutionaries. The hard core of the magazine was a series of biographical essays on republican heroes and extracts from republican literature. It has often been claimed that Behan was one of the chief contributors to *Fianna*,[17] but it is impossible to establish or refute this. Many pieces were anonymous and it is difficult to make attributions on grounds of style when one is dealing with a beginner who is thirteen years old. The fact remains that there is one short story which is signed in Irish, Breandáin Ó Beacháin, and this makes one slow to accept other pieces as his, which are either anonymous or pseudonymous.

'A Tantalising Tale', a story of about seven hundred words, appeared in June 1936. There is no unmistakable stamp of genius about it but it is an interesting performance. The confident opening shows the author combining his literary skills with his political commitments : ' "You ought to have some story worth relating," said the young Kerry O/C as we sat in my library after the Fianna Ard Fheis.' Behan himself is the central figure and, writing out of the bustle of a working-class house, he lavishes the riches of creation on himself. He is an oil-millionaire, who had escaped to America as a rebel but now returns to entertain Fianna delegates in his 'large and comfortable house'. His story concerns a ring he was given in mysterious circumstances while in Paris *'en route* for the USA'. The narrator does not understand the words of the dying donor and finds himself in the hands of the police; however, he produces a pistol and is aboard ship before the police recover. In the USA, he describes his adventure but a search fails to produce the ring. The delegates in Dublin agree that it is a tantalising tale.

Perhaps their verdict is kind : a less sympathetic audience might feel that the author failed to invent a more satisfactory conclusion. Yet if the piece is deficient as a short story, the young author shows a striking poise and a gift for fluid narrative. He assumes the role of the travelled patriotic millionaire with ease, making casual use of what he picked up from books : 'One evening as I strolled along the Rue du Bac, looking out for the house in which Wolfe Tone had stayed . . . I hailed a *fiacre*. . . .' The details come from Wolfe Tone's *Autobiography*. The youngster who wrote the following piece obviously read a great deal and had a natural talent for literary expression : 'Through the good offices of some influential exiles, I obtained a post as monitor in one of the colleges there. One of the Professors there was something of an lapidary and when he heard my tale he asked to see the ring; the stones in it, he said, might possibly have some significance.' The repetition of the phrase 'one of the . . . there' is the only fault.

Republican periodicals tended to be shortlived : *Fianna* ceased publication in 1936 and Behan turned his attention to *Wolfe Tone Weekly* which ran from 1937 till 1939. This was an adult publication which carried current news, patriotic verse, articles on Irish

B

history and serialised extracts from works like Tone's *Autobiography* and Mitchel's *Jail Journal*. Behan's first three contributions were signed—perhaps to compensate for his age, perhaps as a literary gesture—Brendan F. Behan. On 2 October 1937, there was a number of quotations from H. B. C. Pollard's *Secret Societies in Ireland* concerning the Fianna; they had been sent in by 'Brendan F. Behan, Cole and Colley Sluagh, Ath Cliath.' Three weeks later, 'Brendan F. Behan, a 14 years old veteran, recalled a few more things that were said about the Boy Scouts of Ireland.'

It was gratifying to be noticed but he was not content to be a mere reporter of other people's work. In the issue for 2 October he read: '*To 55 poets. Please do not send in any more until you study carefully the verse published in the* Wolfe Tone Weekly *and get an idea of what we want.*' He heeded this advice and saw that the newspaper preferred verse which celebrated the republicans of the past or expressed faith in the republican future or both. His first published stanzas appeared on 8 January 1938: they were introduced as the reply of a 'young boy' to pro-British verses in the *Irish Press*.

> 'Eire'—O God! why do they mock me
> With paper 'freedom'—under England's Crown?
> Even while they forge another link to bind me,
> Another traitor's chain to drag me down.
> But God be praised! My lovers are not vanquished,
> Their arms are strong as steel, their heads are true;
> Another day will see my armies marching
> To strike another blow for Róisín Dubh.
>
> Aye, once again old Dublin will awaken
> To the tramp of marching feet of valiant men;
> The Rearguard will do battle once more for me
> On the mountain, in the town and in the glen.
> Their bayonets shall flash gladly in the sunshine,
> And sycophants and slaves the day will rue,
> When with Judas kiss they put the crown of tinsel
> On the bowed and dear dark head of Róisín Dubh.
>
> My children yet shall drive the foe before them—
> Whether clad in khaki coat or coat of green—
> And mercenaries will flee in droves ere vengeance

O'ertakes them for the insults to their Queen.
My flag shall fly o'er all my many counties—
From Antrim's hills to Kerry's mountains blue—
And my sons shall place the bright gold crown of Freedom
On the dear dark head of deathless Róisín Dubh.

In this piece Behan has followed the editorial line and blended all the standard ingredients—Ireland as Queen-Mother, republicans as lover-sons, the cause as an evangelical crusade against the ungodly—into martial rhetoric. Emotion is stirred up by religious ejaculations, by the usual display of flags, bayonets, crowns and chains, and the solemn tone is insured by the use of *o'er* and *ere*; its appeal is to the converted and there is little behind the verbal and emotional clichés to make it memorable. There is reason to feel that even at the age of fourteen Behan could trot out this sort of thing; it proved a dangerous facility for whenever afterwards he attempted patriotic verse in English he invariably lapsed into banner-waving and sycophant-bashing.[18]

He was more successful when he had some specific image on which to concentrate, as may be seen in *Four Great Names*, published on 24 December 1938. This was almost certainly written on 8 December on the anniversary of four republicans, Rory O'Connor, Liam Mellows, Joseph McKelvey and Richard Barrett, who were shot by the Free State in an act of undisguised vengeance in 1922. The first stanza is promising as it focuses on the actual scene, but the effect is dissipated by the introduction of Mother Ireland and some hackneyed pathetic fallacy.

'Tis midnight, and the only sound the watching sentry's tramp,
December night, frosty, clear, enfolds Mountjoy's armed camp,
Then thunder-like it crashes forth, each word a cry of woe,
These four must die ere morning—Rory, Liam, Dick and Joe.

Proudly they step forward to face the traitors' guns,
O, Ireland, pain is thine tonight but pride in these thy sons,
Four vollies from the rifles held by the green-clad foe
Speed unto God the souls of Rory, Liam, Dick and Joe.

Dear mother, thou are weeping, but gaze not at the night,
See, where morning's crimson rays give hope to Freedom's fight.
And listen to the breezes sigh their message soft and low:
'We'll yet avenge thy loved ones—Rory, Liam, Dick and Joe!'

Such expressions proved Behan's conviction and dedication but the year 1939 showed signs of demanding more than emotional support for the cause. Having waited in vain for the call to arms, he took the boat to Liverpool. Shortly after his arrest he wrote a letter to his uncle Peadar: he was in good spirits and was careful to point out the strong resemblance between the manner of his arrest and that of Tom Clarke, the Fenian who had served sixteen years in England and who had described his experiences in *Glimpses of an Irish Felon's Prison Life*.[19]

2

Freelance 1941-1956

In November 1941, Behan was released from Hollesley Bay Borstal Institution and deported to Ireland; he had only served two years of his three years' sentence and the remission indicates that the British authorities no longer considered him a serious threat. Presumably he was happy to be home again but it was not an unqualified happiness. He had anticipated that his time in England would have made him something of a hero but he soon found that the IRA was not in the mood for hero-worship. The organisation was in shreds: some members had been executed, some had died on hunger-strike, and large numbers were interned. Abroad the bombing campaign had failed; at home security had been so exposed by the police that the IRA Chief of Staff himself, Stephen Hayes, had been suspected of treachery. He was arrested by his own men and pressured into writing a 'confession'. He only escaped a sentence of death by slipping away from them and giving himself up to the Irish police. Despite the new leadership's desire to forget this distasteful business, the Hayes affair caused a serious decline in morale and led to division not only among the active membership but also among IRA men in prison. The loss of cohesion was aggravated by the efforts of some members to form an alliance with Nazi Germany.[1]

This situation must have been particularly disappointing for Behan. Subsequent events suggest that disappointment fostered a sense of insecurity and a desire to prove himself once again. Did he perhaps suspect that some of his comrades doubted the value of his individual attack on England? That remission of sentence for good behaviour cast doubts on his dependability? Did he tell them how he had come to enjoy life at Hollesley Bay and of the friendships he established with some of the English Borstal boys? Or did he concentrate on the cruelty he had experienced in Walton

Jail? There can be little doubt that some inner turmoil inspired his behaviour at Glasnevin Cemetery on 5 April 1942.

It was the day of the annual IRA commemoration of the 1916 insurrection. After the ceremony, members of the Special Branch attempted to arrest three IRA men; one IRA man produced a gun but hesitated to use it. Behan was some distance away but when he saw what was happening he ran towards the man with the gun, screaming at him to use it. When his advice was unheeded, Behan threw off his coat and jacket, grabbed the gun and fired; he fired twice, ran, turned and fired once again and then made off. He was fortunate to get away: one of the detectives was a marksman who decided not to shoot because of the innocent people who crossed his line of fire in panic. After a short time on the run, Behan was arrested, tried and sentenced to fourteen years.

His action on the day of the shooting is a matter of some controversy. It has been suggested that he was drunk and that only an alcoholic haze could have made him do as he did; those who deny this admit that he was highly excited if not hysterical. Behan himself has left an unreliable account of the incident in *Confessions of an Irish Rebel*: everybody except Behan was hysterical, Behan took the revolver apparently to prevent the IRA man from using it, and he only opened fire when the police fired at him. Practically every detail of Behan's story has been shown to be untrue and, perhaps as a reaction against this heroic romance, there has been a tendency to reduce the episode to insignificance.[2] Despite the hysteria and the fanciful emendations there are some hard facts to bear in mind. The introductory paragraph in the *Confessions* rings true: 'The fracas started on our way back from the Cemetery. It was short and sweet like an ass's gallop but in those few moments I lived a full life's span, and in the years that followed I was never to forget them.'[3] The parade of IRA men had been dishearteningly small and showed no desire to confront the police. Most of them had got rid of their weapons. The IRA man holding his fire typified the proceedings. Behan was not immediately concerned and his interference was misconceived. Some irresistible rage overcame him for a moment, forcing him to take over and show himself as the most daring gunman of them all.

The dice were loaded against him. No expert with a gun, he was as likely to hit somebody as miss. If he had killed a detective, he was as good as dead; others had been sentenced to death for attempted murder of police. He was lucky not to be killed or injured as he ran away. While on the run, it seems, he intended to shoot it out with the police rather than allow himself to be taken alive. Officially or unofficially, he was in danger of being shot at sight: the police could not be expected to take chances with him. When one takes into account the temper of the time, he must be considered lucky to have got off with a jail-sentence. It is hardly surprising that for the rest of his life he would continue to hear those shots which reminded him how close he had been to death.

He served less than five years of his sentence, being released under a general amnesty for republicans after the second world war. He retained happy memories of his confinement. He referred to them many years later when inscribing copies of his works for Seán Ó Briain, a fellow-prisoner: 'Locked in prison, we seldom lacked sport and laughter' and 'God be with the old times.'[4] There is a tendency in men to idealise past sufferings but all the evidence suggests that Behan bore his sentence very lightly. He was conspicuous because of his perpetually good humour and his gregariousness. He loved to entertain the others with stories from history or from his own life and fancy.

> It was his telling of the story—making up the play as he went along—never hesitating for a sentence—sometimes inventing very serious conversational passages—plenty of witty cracks and good Dublin humour all mixed together.
>
> No wonder one lad I saw sitting there with his back against the wall had tears of laughter streaming down his face. A sergeant and a few PA's (military police) were shaking with laughter too, and enjoying the drama just as we ourselves were.[5]

The quieter side of his personality did not pass unnoticed: he was known to be a voracious reader, he was applying himself to Irish language and literature and he was also writing a great deal.

He had always had literary ambitions and, like many other prisoners, he found that the discipline of life in jail afforded the time and the concentration necessary for composition. The Governor of Mountjoy was particularly helpful, supplying him with materials and encouragement: he arranged visits by Sean O'Faolain, then editor of *The Bell*, a monthly magazine, eminent writer and former member of the IRA. 'I Become a Borstal Boy', an account of Behan's trial in Liverpool on 8 February 1940, was published in *The Bell* in June 1942. O'Faolain and Behan realised that his experiences in England had provided Behan with the makings of a great book; the IRA leadership in Mountjoy wanted Behan to write a history of the English campaign. Gradually Behan saw that he would have to postpone his novel for a while and concentrate on short stories and plays.[6] He wrote a play, *The Landlady*, based on his Granny English, and there was an effort to have it produced in prison, but some prisoners objected to the language and the references to prostitution and the production was abandoned. Three years later he translated it into Irish and submitted it to the Abbey without success. He also offered the Abbey an early version of the play which would eventually make his name, *The Quare Fellow*, then called *The Twisting of Another Rope*.

The stories he wrote, almost all of which have disappeared, were of three kinds, those which described his time in England, those which dealt with the IRA, and others which were based on childhood memories. In a letter of the time, Behan referred to a story entitled *Borstal Day*. Seamus de Burca, who was close to Behan at the time and who typed out *The Landlady* for him, recalls another story which seems to have been fictional. It told how Behan and another Borstal boy were working as painters and used to have their tea-break with the wife of a warder; nobody in Borstal discussed the offences for which the boys had been sentenced but, eventually, after many conversations, Behan's friend and the warder's wife realise simultaneously that he has murdered her father. De Burca was not particularly impressed by the stories which Behan showed him and only one, 'The Execution', remained vividly fixed in his memory.[7]

The narrator of 'The Execution' is in charge of an IRA party which is to carry out a sentence of death passed on a young Volunteer who, under police pressure, betrayed the location of arms dumps. The narrator feels very sorry for the young lad but accepts the necessity for discipline. There is practically no dialogue, only the command to stop the car and the last request of the victim for time to pray. The style, the stark pared style then associated with Hemingway, is as relentlessly gloomy as the theme. Only once does the narrative deviate slightly from the essential line, when the narrator tries to guess the type of weapon the others are carrying; otherwise the piece is dominated by the one-sentence paragraph.

> We arose and he bent his head—close to his body, as if to avoid a blow.
> I raised my revolver—close to his head—not too close.
> If I put it against his head maybe the muzzle would get blood on it—blood and hair—hair with Brilliantine on it.
> The five guns were levelled at him.
> I cocked mine and pressed slowly on the trigger.

There is little extraneous detail and minimal physical description. The reader follows the robot-like movements of the leader and his morbid fascination with his duty. ' "Letting him have it" "Plugging him" "Knocking him off". It's small wonder people are shy of describing the deed properly— We were going to kill him.' This does not prevent him from shooting: the system demands it. '. . . we couldn't let people give away dumps on us or there'd soon be no respect for the Army . . .' To a great extent, the young lad dies not because anybody desires his death but because the system demands it. The same horrible speculation would later inform Behan's plays. Death is seldom absent from his writings: alone in his cell he had ample time to ponder his own escape at Glasnevin and the precariousness of that vitality which was his chief characteristic.

He was incapable of sustained gloom. He wrote many stories which were set in his own childhood and which were dominated by the dialect of the northside. Seán Ó Briain recalled one about a trip to Howth during which one *oul wan* described the battle fought at Clontarf in 1014 between King Brian Boru and the Vikings:

> Them Danes fellows—after the fighting was all over—killed poor Brian Boru himself—a King he was Mrs Jewel, a real King. The poor old man be all accounts saying his prayers— over there near the Bull—when this Dane fellow—Brooder be name, I heard me oul one say, and she knew—a pagan he was —a real pagan she said—up he comes behind poor old Brian Boru's back and cuts the head offa him and as I was saying he was there someplace alongside the Bull saying his prayers . . .

In these efforts Behan was transcribing the stories he told so well. He shared with the people of the northside an ability to rescue history from academic seriousness and to resuscitate those who had become—for others—mere names, seeing them in terms of the life around them. The Invincibles were a group of Dublin artisans who carried out a double assassination in the Phoenix Park in 1882. Behan's account of the operation owes more to the oral traditions of Dublin's northside than it does to academic research. There, Skin-the-Goat, a jarvey, remained as real a person as he was to those in the cabman's shelter in *Ulysses*. ' "Joe Brady," says he, "I think I seen that man moving." Joe goes back and finishes the job. "That's right," says Skin-the-Goat, "A dead cock doesn't crow." '[8] Historians may doubt whether this conversation ever took place but nobody can deny that Behan has dramatised the situation in an utterly convincing and macabre manner.

> When I knew I was going to be free again, I knew that I was going to be free again to hunger and to poverty and to no kind of pyjamas, not even the Free State Army ones.[9]

Behan was among the last republicans to be released under a general amnesty in the winter of 1946/47, one of the longest and coldest winters on record. He was almost twenty-four and had spent most of the previous six years in prison on political charges; that he should find some difficulty in adapting to his new status was inevitable, for his personality had been to a great extent moulded by imprisonment. It would probably be an overstatement to say that Behan enjoyed confinement but it is clear that he regarded it with unusual equanimity. There was no question of him being ashamed of being imprisoned for political reasons; he was, if anything, proud of it. After his time in Walton, he would have found the life of a republican prisoner in Ireland relatively comfortable. Within the limits of the prison he was allowed to move about and mingle with his fellow-prisoners quite freely. Among his IRA colleagues he found many congenial companions who appreciated his social talents and there were some to whom he could confide his dream of being a great Irish writer. Prison afforded him a higher education which he would not have had on the outside because of the financial circumstances of his family: classes were arranged in a number of subjects and there was ample time for reading and discussion. Above all, prison gave him the chance to write copiously and at his ease—an advantage enjoyed only by the wealthy outside. In prison he lived among people who shared his views on politics and on writing and who were always there to encourage, advise and criticise. For one who was passionately keen to excel as a writer, prison offered a form of patronage, if only bed and board; Behan knew that once outside he would be expected to work as a housepainter in order to survive and that this would involve living with tradesmen who, though ideal as mates, would have no sympathetic understanding of his literary ambitions. Once outside he would miss more than the prison pyjamas.

Behan's life over the next few years was very confused. He sometimes worked as a painter in various parts of the country but he was not a dependable employee for he came to hate more and more the work which testified to his lack of progress as a writer. He was unable to bury his ambitions and unwilling to inflict his unpaid genius on his family. He frequented a literary pub off Grafton Street and soon became part of the Bohemian circle of which it was the focus. He was welcomed and applauded but not as a writer; he was a performer, wit, raconteur, and his working class and prison background made him appear all the more extravagant and bizarre to the others. He welcomed appreciation of any kind but behind the stream of jokes he was desperately conscious of his inability to dedicate himself to writing.[10] He was trying. To *The Bell* he sent an account of the IRA training camp in Killiney but the editor, Peadar O'Donnell who was sympathetic to him, rejected it on the grounds that it did justice neither to Behan himself nor to the others mentioned.[11] He occasionally wrote poems in Irish which were published in *Comhar* but these were not sufficient to give him a sense of fulfilment. He undertook to write a play for an IRA concert and did so in two days; neither the concert nor the play was a success and Behan was too drunk to take the part he had rehearsed.[12]

In March 1947 he was again in prison in England. He was involved in an attempt to free an IRA prisoner from an English jail. There is again some dispute as to the extent of his involvement but there can be no doubt as to the combination of bravery, foolhardiness and sheer inefficiency he displayed: the prisoner got back to Ireland but Behan was arrested and sentenced to four months.[13]

Eventually he returned to his divided life in Dublin, to the 'death without dignity' of painting and the escapist hilarity of the literary set, to the admiration of the crowded bar and the inner fear that he would never make it as a writer. Friends noticed an element of desperation in his drinking which, in retrospect, is not surprising. In August 1948 he was back in Mountjoy for assaulting a policeman while on a binge; this time he wore prison clothes and the sentence included hard labour. When, shortly after being released, he heard that a friend was going to Paris, he decided to get away from Ireland. Paris had the reputation of being an artist's city and many writers had served their apprenticeship there. It might be what he needed: perhaps he could lose himself and his reputation in a new city and release the artist in himself.

He never really settled in Paris but he spent a good deal of time there over the next two years; nor did the change of place prove the panacea he was looking for. Shortage of money led him to take a series of jobs, including painting and smuggling. He became acquainted with a group of Americans who were also writing but Paris was too interesting and money too scarce to enable Behan to establish an industrious routine. If he sought in Paris a release from the social pressures which plagued him in Dublin he was disappointed: even here he was forced to take up odd jobs and the change of atmosphere did nothing to prevent him from drinking heavily. Eventually, most of his acquaintances thought 'he was just a bloody drunken show-off Irishman, the sort that is caricatured'.[14] Yet, if Paris did not work any miracles, it was not without its effect. Initially, the Paris literary set had been more understanding than its Dublin counterpart and had treated him as one of themselves. Behan's growing confidence in his talent may be gauged from two short stories which he published in 1950, the year he returned to Ireland with a new determination.

Sometime I will explain to you the feeling of isolation one suffers writing in a Corporation housing scheme.[15]

Those who lived in Corporation houses were working-class and it was expected that they would work as labourers or tradesmen. Writing was not an accepted trade and the ambition to write was looked upon as disastrous from the economic point of view and arrogant from the social point of view. Only a rich family could afford the luxury of a writer, while most of those who practised as writers did not depend on writing for their living. Because of his unwillingness to abandon literature for house-painting Behan was something of an outcast among the people he loved most, working-class Dubliners. Possibly because they were his favourite people, Behan was never accepted as a writer by the other circle in which he moved, the largely middle-class group of artists and associates who frequented the pub off Grafton Street. The 'feeling of isolation' which he experienced is objectified in the two stories of 1950.

'A Woman of No Standing', published in the Dublin magazine, *Envoy*, in August 1950, describes a broken marriage. From the outset, the style is dramatic, apparently uncontrived and immediate:

> 'And the priest turns round to me' says Ria, 'and says he: "But you don't mean to say that this person still goes down to see him?" '

Ulick O'Connor wrote that the story is 'seen through the eyes of a little boy' but this is not so; the narrator orders drinks after the funeral and generally speaks as an adult, most likely a woman.[16]

> We had a few prayers that night, but she never turned up, and I was sorry, because to tell the truth, I was curious to see her . . . Ria had the hearse go round the block where we'd all lived years ago—happy, healthy, though riotous times—fighting being better than loneliness.

The narrative style is disarmingly simple: the tale is told with minimal reflection or comment in what strikes the reader as a transcription of Dublin working-class speech.

Ria's husband, who separated from her when their daughter was five, is now dying in hospital where he is still visited by 'the other woman'—much to the disgust of his wife and child and to the horror of a priest who sees to it that the visits are forbidden. At the funeral all eyes look out for her. The narrator assumes that she is a rich prostitute: 'I had some idea of a big car (owned by a new and tolerant admirer) sweeping into the cortege from some side street or another, or else a cab that'd slide in, a woman in rich mourning heavily veiled in its corner.' But she sees instead 'a woman of no standing', a poorly dressed middle-aged woman who has been 'scrubbing halls for me dear departed this last four years—since he took bad'.

The story is slight but effectively produced. The narrator, a friend of the wife, accepts the general attitude of condemnation, but she is unable to conceal her shock at the disparity between the glamorous whore of her imagination and the poor creature who stands on the edge of the funeral as a social leper. Intuitively and perhaps unwillingly the narrator feels for the forbidden lover and begins to suspect that the scrubbing of halls was an expression of a love much deeper than the wounded respectability of the widow. In choosing to allow us to follow events through the sharp eye and limited mind of an anonymous neighbour, Behan showed remarkable subtlety. The narrator is bound in friendship to the aggrieved wife and shares her obedience to the moral climate and its controller, the priest. Although in her heart she is capable of tolerance, she is intellectually unable to resolve her mixed feelings. She embodies the prejudices which damn 'the other woman' but she is never totally alienated from the reader. The story ends on a note of pity not only for 'the woman of no standing' but for all the characters involved.

'After the Wake' appeared in the Paris-based *Points* in December 1950. Towards the end of his career, when Behan was unable to supply books for which he had already been paid, his publishers excavated earlier stories and poems. 'A Woman of No Standing' and 'The Confirmation Suit' re-emerged in *Brendan Behan's Island*. 'After the Wake', although probably the finest story he ever wrote, was left in the relative obscurity of *Points*, almost certainly because its homosexual theme would not have fitted in with the public personality which Behan was projecting. It would have come as a shock to most people to learn that he could write so understandingly on such a subject. Today, neither the theme nor style surprise; what is striking is the sustained mastery of tone and structure. 'After the Wake' and 'A Woman of No Standing' may be taken as companion pieces and not merely because they appeared in the same year: the titles are interchangeable, they are both based on the eternal triangle and both describe forbidden love in a working-class Dublin context.

'After the Wake' tells how the narrator, a young man who lives in a tenement, sets out to seduce a married man who lives on a floor beneath him. When the wife goes into hospital, the narrator 'opened the campaign in jovial earnest'. He had already done some groundwork—lending them a book on homosexuality, sitting close beside him after swimming, 'our bare thighs touching', discussing with him the inconvenience of living in tenements where one had to sleep with one's brother. Her operation for cancer is unsuccessful and she dies hours afterwards. The wake involves heavy drinking and, when all the others have gone, the narrator helps the widower to bed.

> I had to almost carry him to the big double bed in the inner room.
> I first loosened his collar to relieve the flush on his smooth cheeks, took off his shoes and socks and pants and shirt, from the supple muscled thighs, the stomach flat as an altar boy's and noted the golden smoothness of the blond hair on every part of his firm white flesh.
> I went to the front room and sat by the fire till he called me.
> 'You must be nearly gone yourself,' he said, 'you might as well come in and get a bit of rest.'
> I sat on the bed, undressing myself by the faint flickering of the candles from the front room.

The outline gives little indication of the complexity of a story which is a masterpiece of tragi-comedy, based on the ambivalence of the narrator.

He is genuinely fond of both husband and wife: 'I'd complimented them, individually and together, on their being married to each other—and I meant it.' So obvious is his affection that it is noticed and translated by neighbours into the standard form: 'From that day forward I was cast as her unfortunate admirer, my jealousy of him sweetened by my friendship for them both.' On the night before she goes into hospital they drink together and when the narrator sings a love-song, she breaks down: she *knows* that he has been singing his love for her and she *knows* that her husband does not mind. She also pities the narrator. ' "Because, God help you," she said to me, "that never knew anything better than going down town half-drunk and dirty rotten bitches taking your last farthing." ' At the wake, several people hint at the love he had for her, 'giving me an understanding smile and licence to mourn my pure unhappy love.' This undercurrent is never refuted by the narrator: the mood of the story is not one of simple conquest but rather one of confused melancholy. Throughout there is a sad awareness that for his love he must live a lie, working 'cautiously and steadily' in the alien atmosphere of his native place. He must prepare his propaganda, carefully arguing how ordinary and manly is the love of one man for another while hiding his mind from all but him. There is even a hint of uncertainty: 'On the other hand, appealing to that hope of culture—Socrates, Shakespeare—Marlowe—lies, truth and half-truth.'

The style is a development of the stark style of 'The Execution', more highly organised to reflect the quiet torture within the narrator's mind, but essentially simple, unpretentious, confidential. The references to books and writers in a tenement room show part of the attempt to break away from the common culture. There are, perhaps, two moments when the tone changes slightly from dominant gentle melancholy. The first works well and captures the wave of nausea which attacks the narrator as he looks at the corpse whose incipient decay has given new life to his desire.

> It is a horrible thing how quickly death and disease can work on a body.
>
> She didn't look like herself any more than the brown parchment thin shell of a mummy looks like an Egyptian warrior.
>
> Worse than the mummy, for he at least is dry and clean as dust. Her poor nostrils were plugged with cotton-wool and her mouth hadn't closed properly, but showed two front teeth, like a rabbit's.

The effect of the final paragraph is doubtful. It follows on the fine picture of the narrator sitting on the double bed, undressing by the flickering light of the candles which surround the coffin in the other room, and it poses a problem for the reader: 'I fancied her face looking up from the open coffin, on the Americans who, having imported wakes from us, invented morticians themselves.' Perhaps the change of tone is intended as a smile of success? But where are the Americans? If the conclusion is flawed it is all the more unfortunate coming so late in a story which had been superbly controlled throughout.

In other ways too, 1950 was an important year for Behan. Two of his poems were included in *Nuabhéarsaíocht*, an anthology of contemporary Irish verse: he was accepted as a sensitive talent by a small section of the reading public. Despite the advances he was making in the short story and lyric, he was unsatisfied. In one of the *Nuabhéarsaíocht* poems, '*Guí an Rannaire*', he seemed to accept that he would never be a great poet, and he subsequently wrote very little verse; nor did he ever again write stories in the quiet vein of 'After the Wake'. From 1950 onwards he set his sights on two major works, his novel on Borstal and his play which dealt with a hanging. He was not the kind of person who could be content with the quiet approval which greets a poem in Irish or a short story in a little magazine. From earliest childhood he had craved the glamour of adulation; he had always longed to make some noise in the world. Hence his ill-advised journey to Liverpool in 1939, the affair at Glasnevin in 1942, and his life-long inability to resist an audience. There was, beside this, a quieter self—most clearly seen in the poet of an obscure tongue—but from 1950 onwards this began to recede beyond recognition. The economic problem remained but shortly after his return from France he gradually established himself as a freelance journalist and earned his living by writing rather than painting. Such employment left him more time to press on with his more serious work.

Comhar, the magazine in which most of his poetry had appeared, was sympathetic. Behan proposed a book in Irish about his prison experiences and *Comhar* subsidised a stay in Connemara to improve his Irish. Some drafts were submitted, but no final copy.[17] In April 1951 there appeared in *Comhar* a lighthearted piece by Behan entitled 'Na hOilithrigh' (The Pilgrims), which offers insight into his personality. The story tells how Behan (appearing as himself as he was increasingly wont to do in his writings) and an unnamed poet were in the south of France on their way to Rome. While the poet was anxious to sniff the intellectual atmosphere of Europe, Behan was happy wherever there was drink and conversation. The poet lost his patience.

'Always drink! Drink! Drink! You think of nothing else.'
'I do,' said I, eager to list the other subjects of my contemplation in self-defence.
'O, you're the great fellow. The big man of the Studio Bar, the big man of McDaid's in Harry Street, the life and soul of the Mabillon roaring round the place like a drunken bull. *You'll*

introduce me to writers, the crowd in the Cafe de Flore, *you'll* take me drinking with the boys of the Beaux Arts. And in the heel of the hunt who are you? An ignorant animal from a Dublin back-street with nothing to distinguish you from the other thousands of them except that your tongue is more obscene and your lungs stronger.'

His anger expressed, the poet feared Behan would leave him there on the road, which is precisely what Behan did. What strikes the reader today is the self-portrait which Behan offers of himself: he makes no attempt to refute the poet's allegations. Perhaps at the time of writing Behan thought that he had scored over the poet by showing him to be frightened of journeying alone and by accusing the poet of the kind of prejudice which Behan suspected in the Dublin literary set; today, however, it is tempting to see the argument as between two elements of Behan's own personality, the artist and the entertainer.

Later in 1951, Riobard Mac Góráin became editor of *Comhar* and proposed that Behan should write something about the IRA. There was no visit to Connemara this time and Behan did produce six articles entitled *Pléascáin i Sasana* (Bombs in England) which set out to present an objective account of the 1939 bombing campaign. The objectivity was not sustained and the spotlight soon fell on the involvement of one IRA Volunteer named Brendan Behan, on the republican tradition of his family and on his training in Killiney Castle. Unfortunately, there was no description of his subsequent imprisonment, perhaps because he was already working on this in English.[18]

He wrote some programmes for the national radio station in 1951 and this led Mícheál Ó hAodha to invite him to take part in a series called *The Balladmakers' Saturday Night*. He wrote scripts for the Dublin sections and sang as well. With his fine singing voice and his collection of songs and stories, it was easy money but, apart altogether from the fee, these programmes gained him a wide audience and helped to impress his name on the general public. He hoped that his play, *The Twisting of Another Rope*, would be accepted for radio production, although apparently he had no fair copy of the script. Ó hAodha saw Behan's talent for dramatic character but thought his technique weak. He suggested that Behan should try his hand at imitating a successful series of domestic comedy, *The Foley Family*. As a result, two episodes, *Moving Out* and *A Garden Party* were broadcast in 1952.[19] Both are based on the movement of the Behan family from Russell Street to the new suburbs; they are very professionally done but whatever lasting value they have is due to the colourful use of the city dialect. Behan picked up the tricks of the freelancer's trade very quickly and became highly efficient in the production of required material for newspaper, magazine or radio. Gradually he came to realise that he had an almost limitless amount of material and a highly personal brand of it: all he had to do was recall some episode from his past and describe it in the lively language he had cultivated all his life. This released his essentially convivial personality and the mix was ideal for a newspaper article. There were other kinds of freelancing to which he was not quite suited. All his insecurities emerged when he was given the task of interviewing and consequently he drank a great deal, sufficient to worry even himself.

Two works which appeared in 1953 were almost certainly written simply to make money; the high standard they achieve shows just how well Behan could write in this atmosphere. 'The Confirmation Suit', his last short story, is radically different in tone from his earlier efforts.[20] In place of the anonymous narrator and (for the most part) the stark muted style, one now encounters the young Brendan Behan himself: the texture is rich with psychological and linguistic oddities and the binding force is the disarmingly boyish character of Brendan himself. He is not mentioned by name but there is little attempt to disguise the setting in Russell Street and cast of the Behans and their neighbours. (Behan's teacher, Sister Monica, and his step-brothers, Rory and Seán, are mentioned by name.) One quarter of the story, generally irrelevant to the subject of confirmation, is devoted to Behan's grandmother, 'a lady of capernosity and function. She had money and lay in bed all day, drinking porter or malt, and taking pinches of snuff, and talking to the neighbours that would call up and tell her the news of the day.' She is the victim of improving visits from Aunt Jack, a believer in cleanliness and an admirer of the cheap nourishment in sheep's heads. Granny was forced to sample one but did not relish it: 'When she took it out of the pot and laid it on the plate, she and I sat looking at it, in fear and trembling. It was bad enough going into the pot, but with the soup streaming from its eyes, and its big teeth clenched in a very bad temper, it would put the heart crossways in you.' Young Brendan is requested to fling the offensive head out the window and Granny restores her spirits with a drink.

Nominally, the story tells of the suit which was made for Brendan's confirmation by one Miss McCann, habit-maker. The style of the suit is so unfashionable that the young boy is ashamed to be seen in it; he decides to hide it always beneath the overcoat which was bought in a shop. In the heat of the crowded church he passes out—just as he is about to pledge himself to abstain from alcoholic drinks—and he only wears the suit for a few minutes every Sunday when he visits Miss McCann. Eventually his mother tells Miss McCann, causing the habit-maker to cry. Shortly afterwards Miss McCann dies and, despite rain and cold, the young boy walks behind her coffin without his overcoat, showing his confirmation suit to the world. In summary the story seems to deal with the pain of adolescence and it is not without sentimentality at the close but, taken as a whole, it is much more jovial. The story is essentially a peg on which Behan hangs a series of characters who come from a world of surrealistic comedy. The reader is introduced into this world by the boy himself, the tough guy who is more than a little afraid of the confirmation ritual, living in fear of appearing in the livery of poverty, jersey and pants, his vanity smouldering beneath the indignity of the eccentric suit, his sense of decency eventually breaking through his selfishness. Most of the raw material and the lively language may be traced back to Behan's own childhood in Russell Street but, with undeniable skill and imagination, he has infused into local memory the bubbling spirit of comedy.

On 19 October 1953, the *Irish Times* carried the first of thirty instalments of a serial, *The Scarperer*, by Emmet Street. Behan later claimed that he had used this pseudonym to fool the literary intelligentsia of Dublin who despised him as a writer of pornography, but this is not very convincing.[21] It seems more likely that he himself was so eager to discard the image of hack journalist and to be accepted as a serious writer that he was afraid to put his name to a lightweight newspaper serial. He was painfully aware that, despite his poems, short stories and work in progress, he was still better known as a freelance journalist and 'character'. To be seen to write a crime fiction serial would have aggravated the imbalance which he hoped to correct with his more serious work. *The Scarperer*, he knew, was written for money and, at this stage, he probably lacked the confidence to accept it as such and judge it on its merits. Those who were not well disposed towards him could point to the serial and ask aloud if this was the great work of which he had spoken; Behan knew that it was not but he also knew that the great work had yet to be completed and published.

Though no masterpiece, *The Scarperer* reads easily and well. It is the work of a professional writer. The highly convoluted plot is delivered with excellent control and it is difficult to imagine anybody anticipating the reason for the failure of the criminal plan which is the basis of the story. Behan also makes maximum use of his specialist knowledge. He knew the inside of Mountjoy Jail in Dublin and the atmosphere of the pubs where the criminal fringe drank; he had also indulged in smuggling between France and Ireland and had lived in Paris. The story involves the freeing of a prisoner from Mountjoy and his transportation to France— via the Aran Islands where Behan actually wrote the serial. The prisoner is chosen not merely because he is willing to pay but also because of his resemblance to a top French criminal who will pay a fortune to have what appears to be his body found drowned by the French police. Despite the credibility of the dialogue and the locations, the *dénouement* brings the tale into the realm of farce: the perfect plan is spoiled—accidentally—by Irish women campaigning against the live export of Irish horses to France. The author's merriment shows in his having the crucial recognition take place in front of a poster advertising a lecture on WHAT MAKES THINGS HAPPEN.[22]

Throughout, *The Scarperer* had been a strange mixture of comedy and criminal violence. In the Shaky Man's pub are the hilarious inhabitants of Behan's city. There is Tralee Trembles, son of 'one of the biggest pig-blockers in Castle Island', ex-schoolmaster, poet, wine-victim and subject of diabolical hallucinations. There is also Mr O'Donnell, whose Christian name is Pig's Eye and who organises the lottery. The alcoholic cheer of the pub is tempered by the appearance of Eddie Collins; soon afterwards one of the raucous women, Nancy Hand, meets a stranger. Kilbeggan Kate relates: "She went down the street to meet some fellow. He put it on her. Shivved her. Razor. Anything to do tonight? No? Well," she [Kate] made the gesture of a sharp instrument drawn across the face, "sew that up." '[23] People learn that there is a time to sing and a time to shut up; a mistake means a beating, a slashing, or even death. Despite the combination of high farce and stark realism, only once does the narrative lose its pace and direction: when the prisoners are being transported to Mountjoy. Although the author's attention should fix on Tralee Trembles, he chooses to show us the effect of imprisonment through the eyes of a young boy who is inside for the first time. It is possible that Behan did this consciously, that he looked for a credible means of describing the jail in a work which does not normally delay on physical description; however, it is more likely that he was side-tracked because, at the time, he was much more interested in the other novel he was writing, *Borstal Boy*, the main theme of which was the effect of imprisonment on a young boy.

During these years Behan's interest in prison was not entirely imaginative: in 1952 he was sentenced in England for breaking the deportation order which was still in effect against him, and in 1954 he was back in Mountjoy for being drunk and disorderly. The court appearance which was most helpful was during the libel action brought by Patrick Kavanagh against the *Leader* magazine. Kavanagh was convinced, mistakenly, that Behan had written the offensive article and, in the extensive coverage of the case, Behan's name was widely advertised. The case, thought hilarious at the time, seems rather sordid today: Kavanagh's artistic aloofness became rather unattractive under cross-examination and eventually he was made to look ridiculous. His claim to have always hated Behan was not helped when one of his books, cordially inscribed to Behan, was produced in court. By the time the trial was over, few readers of Irish newspapers were unacquainted with the name of Brendan Behan. Perhaps the tide was turning: early in 1954 he was sufficiently satisfied with his play to send it to the Abbey, where it was rejected, and he also began what was to become a regular column in the *Irish Press*.

On Monday 8 February, an article appeared in the *Press* under the headline 'Brendan Behan remembers'. This was an account of the countryside around Dublin during his childhood. After a short interval, the column developed into a Saturday feature: initially it dealt with the North of Ireland, then Paris, and, on 22 May, the readers of the *Press* met Mrs Brennan and Mr

Crippen who were to be regulars. These short pieces, many of them dashed off with speed in order to qualify the author for an advance, were extremely popular at the time and, later on, in 1963, a selection was published entitled *Hold Your Hour and Have Another*. The essays range from childhood reminiscences to the goings-on in Michael's pub, from accounts of Behan's travels to commentary on current events. They are all informed by the personality of the author, who often appears demurely in Michael's pub, generous, loquacious, inoffensively proud of his travels, an unfanatical supporter of the working-class people who comprised the majority of his readers and a conscientious objector to the work undertaken by that class. As ephemeral journalism few of the pieces were not outstandingly fresh and lively. Many of those included in *Hold Your Hour and Have Another* have improved with age because they preserve something of a world which has passed away.

Chief among these are the pieces which celebrate the hedonistic spirit of the people Behan saw as a child, the inhabitants of old Dublin who, with their British Army pensions, had no official part to play in the Irish Free State. There were others who were anything but supporters of the British Army, whose contributions to Irish separatism had been lost sight of because their urban traditions did not meet with the approval of the new, essentially rural, cultural establishment. Behan made no bones about his affection for the traditions which came down from 'the unregenerate pre-Gaelic League people'.[24] He loved the company of the older folk who were in touch with those times and he found them in the early-opening pubs in the city markets. It is because so many of the articles capture the spirit of Mrs Brennan and Maria Concepta in rhythm and image that they ring true in all their surrealistic glory. The late fusilier Brennan once punched a countryman in the ankle for asking if he was a child or a midget. Brennan escaped from the enemy during the Boer War by wearing a busby: they thought he was a hedgehog. Mrs Brennan is a lover of Irish songs such as that sung by Maria Concepta:

A sound as of a death-rattle came from under her shawl, and then, without further warning, a most blood-curdling moan went through the shop, as she threw back her covering and bayed the ceiling.

'Howl, howl, *howl* . . .'

The cat glanced anxiously round and at the third note got down from the window and ran out the door.

'You never lost it,' said Crippen, nodding his head in appreciation.

Maria Concepta screwed up her face another bit, and went on 'Howl! How long will dear old Ireland be unfree?'

'Lovely,' muttered Mrs Brennan, rapping on the counter, and humming to herself. ' "Oh, never marry a soldier, an airman or a maree-ing, if you can get a rebel in his uniform of greeing." '[25]

Mr Crippen is, in his own words, 'one of the dead who died for Ireland'. Hero of many engagements, he is a verbal artist, composing the most intricate betting-slips while not composing verse. Hovering on the edge of things is Brending Behing, the budding genius with his Rennington typewriter, his weight considerably increased since he gave up work: his attempts at wit are invariably disastrous.

There are some tall tales from the author's childhood. On one occasion he helped a theatrical relation by appearing on stage as 'the blind, singing, crippled newsboy'. On another he showed his early gregariousness and dramatic talent. It happened when he was at a performance of the film of *Gallipoli* in which many Dublin Fusiliers are seen meeting their doom.

From every part of the gods the screeches went up, 'Oh, there's our Mickser.' Other old ones screeched: 'Oh, take me out, I can't stick it. There's me husband in the water.'

Granny Carmody was not to be bested and let a roar out of her that you'd hear in Gallipoli.

'Oh, me own sweet onion, there he is, me poor first husband's brother.'

As the face that appeared close up at that moment was that of a bearded Indian, I was very much impressed by the Granny's relations.

'Oh, there's me da.' I let out a roar for the good reason that you might as well be out of the world as out of the fashion.

'Ah, God help the poor child,' some old one screamed from behind, 'he's gone into a wakeness.' I wasn't, until she put the idea into my head and then I did and moaned, 'Da, da, da.'[26]

To help him recover, he is given tea and cakes in the manager's office which all goes to prove the inherent—if slightly irregular—virtue of the world in which these adventures are situated.

Behan's major breakthrough came when his play, now renamed *The Quare Fellow*, was produced at the tiny Pike Theatre in late 1954. In February 1955 he married and this introduced a new stability and regularity into his life which helped him to write consistently. In January 1956, *The Quare Fellow* was accepted by the Theatre Royal, Stratford East, London, and the production that summer made Brendan Behan a household name in Britain. His unfinished book on Borstal was accepted by a leading London publisher, the BBC commissioned a radio play, Gael Linn commissioned a play in Irish. He had arrived, had hit the big time: everybody wanted him to write for them, anything at all. In 1956 he gave up writing his column for the *Irish Press*.

3

Behan's Irish Poetry

Behan first achieved literary prominence as a poet in Irish: he was the youngest author represented in *Nuabhéarsaíocht*, a collection of modern Irish poetry edited by Seán Ó Tuama in 1950. Máirtín Ó Cadhain, arguably the greatest writer of Irish in this century, reckoned that among those whose work was included in *Nuabhéarsaíocht* there were two genuine poets, one of whom was Behan.[1] Within two years of this recognition he had written his last poem.

His output was small—a dozen short lyrics—but sufficiently strong to merit reassessment today.[2] Nor is it only the intrinsic merit of the verse which engages attention. His career as an Irish poet prompts two questions. Why did he write poetry in a language which was not his vernacular? And why, having done so well, did he stop? It must have been obvious to one of his upbringing that a poet in Irish wrote for a tiny fraction of the population, and that a national revival of the language was, despite the optimism of enthusiasts, a dim prospect. The native speaker may argue that Irish is the only medium for him, and others, less plausibly, that though it be a secondary and acquired language for them, it is, for historical reasons, the one best equipped to express the imagination of an Irish writer. Some writers have sought in the Irish language and tradition an alternative to what they saw as the sterility of mid-Atlantic English culture, and it is fashionable today to translate from the Irish, partly, no doubt, in search of technical novelty, partly in reaction to loss of identity in the contemporary world. One fact is undeniable. The writer who chooses to work in Irish rather than in English is seeking something other than popularity: he may write great verse, but must leave it to a little clan.

Neither of Behan's parents knew more than a few words of Irish but they used them with pride, teaching their children to respect the language as an aspect of that national independence to which they were committed. The gifts which people noticed in the young Brendan were those which would have facilitated language-learning: a fine ear, a prodigious memory and a talent for mimicry. He was probably being falsely modest when he alluded to 'the bit of Irish' he knew as a result of his formal schooling.[3] As he graduated from the Fianna to the IRA he had ample opportunity to meet fluent Irish speakers. Although not all members of the IRA could speak Irish, the movement gave it unqualified support and there were close links and overlapping membership between the IRA and organisations more specifically dedicated to cultural affairs. In republican circles Behan encountered native speakers, musicians, and storytellers. His higher education in Irish took place during his imprisonment from 1942 to 1946, his studies directed by teachers who knew by heart an amount of poetry and poetic lore which seems incredibly extensive to those whose education has been through books rather than through oral transmission. Almost as important as the availability of teachers was the special atmosphere among republican prisoners and internees. IRA men maintained some sense of discipline and community while confined: in the classes which they organised themselves, many read at least as rewardingly as they would have in an educational institution.[4]

Behan was particularly fortunate to find among his fellow-prisoners in Mountjoy Seán Ó Briain, a schoolteacher from Bally-ferriter in the Irish-speaking part of County Kerry. It was in Seán Ó Briain's company that he acquired the ability to converse in Irish with something of the ease and copiousness of a native speaker. He also learned a lot of the poetry and social history of Gaelic Ireland. In describing his own birthplace for Behan, Ó Briain conjured up an Ireland worth fighting for. The barrier of language had enabled the people of the Kerry *Gaeltacht* to preserve a cultural continuity of which the greater part of the country had been deprived. Successive waves of invaders had been absorbed and had become as Irish as the original inhabitants. In this close-knit community Behan could see a Gaelic version of his own area in northside Dublin. The people were proud of themselves and their descent, of the history in song and story which they handed from generation to generation. Behan was attracted to the apparent classlessness and the absence in Irish of a system of accents de-

noting social status which a working-class Dubliner could not fail
to notice in English. These people had produced and treasured
the princely Piaras Feiritéir and the rakish Eoghan Rua Ó Súil-
leabháin. Ó Briain's picture enchanted Behan: it epitomised with
a new clarity the ideal to which he had dedicated himself from
childhood, an Irish society which had proudly maintained a cultural
identity impervious to British colonial abuse.

Behan's immersion in the Irish language coincided with the
beginning of his adult career as a writer. There were growing-
pains. He was uncomfortably aware of contradictions within himself, between his republican idealism and his own experiences in
England, between his duties as a soldier and his ambitions as a
writer. The Irish language offered a possible resolution: were he
to write in Irish he could follow his own private inclinations while
at the same time continuing his part in the struggle against British
imperialism. It is interesting to consider to what extent did his
commitment to Irish influence his writings as a whole. During
these years he acquired a discipline which never came easily to
him, the ability to transmute into quiet industry those elements of
his personality which craved public performance; between 1942
and 1946 he began to work towards his two masterpieces, *The
Quare Fellow* and *Borstal Boy*.[5] To a great extent the cell in
Mountjoy facilitated this, but perhaps even more influential
was the focusing of aim and energy on the demands of Irish
literature.

Early in 1944 Behan was transferred to the Curragh where he
encountered Máirtín Ó Cadhain who used his period of internment to read, write, study and teach. Ó Cadhain was concerned
with the feasibility of a modern Irish literature. A brilliant control
of language was not enough, he argued; unless there was creative
talent nobody would read simply for the sake of the language.
He was aware of the revival of interest in Irish writing but was
sceptical: 'Those who begin to write in a language they don't
know and which they do not try to learn properly have an awful
cheek. I myself could write English better than most of them—
most of this crowd who are writing in Irish without knowing it.'[6]
The revival was not confined to republican prisoners but was a
national phenomenon. In his introduction to *Nuabhéarsáíocht*,
Seán Ó Tuama was to write:

In future when people try to establish when the development of modern Irish poetry began, they will probably settle for 1939. In that year, Conradh na Gaeilge resumed the Oireachtas competitions in Dublin; at the same time the second world war began. It would be difficult to decide if those events had a greater influence than the founding of the universities' magazine, *Comhar*, three years later; yet this much is certain: the resurgence of national feeling in this country during the war brought a proportionate re-awakening of interest in writing; and in the case of poetry, this revival was developed and assisted to a considerable extent by the Oireachtas competitions and by the Irish-language periodicals, especially *Comhar*.[7]

The writers involved saw that their basic problem was that of using the resources of Irish to create a medium which would suit modern poetry, increasingly urban in its preoccupations. Yet most of the writers—and all of those who were native speakers—came from rural backgrounds and inherited a poetic tradition which was untouched by the twentieth-century city. All poets must to some extent expand language to embrace their imaginative discoveries but the problem was unusually pressing for the Irish poet. For the non-native speaker the need for expansion was coupled with that of acquisition, while in all cases there was some element of doubt as to the survival of the language as a modern tongue. After three years of writing in English and learning Irish, Behan took the obvious first step towards writing in Irish, translation. He sent a version of *The Landlady* and an early draft of *The Quare Fellow* to the Abbey Theatre.[8]

Towards the end of Behan's time in the Curragh, Seán McCaughey, an IRA leader, died on hunger-strike in Portlaoise. The December issue of *Comhar* contained a poem by Behan which commemorated McCaughey's self-sacrifice. Entitled 'The Return of McCaughey', it concentrates not on the physical death but on the spiritual triumph as seen in the return of the remains to Belfast. The ballad captures the victory of mind over matter. The second stanza:

I had expected to witness a funeral
With pipes of condolence droning their keen,
Had thought that the sound of guns would be mournful,
But, like the victorious host of O'Neill,
Come from the Pale having crushed the invader,

The Gaels are delighted to carry their trophy,
To welcome McCaughey back home to Ulster,
For pride is eventually stronger than woe.[9]

Taken on its own terms—as a celebration of glorious death—it is quite successful, full of zest and colour. There are loosenesses of expression which might have been tidied up, and the three and a half stanzas would suggest that the author ran out of steam and did not bother to reorganise what he had written, but the poem is essentially rhetorical and is more concerned with atmosphere than with argument. As the work of a beginner it is remarkably fluent in movement and sound-pattern, an *ambrán*[10] rather than a translation.

In January 1947 Behan walked in the funeral of Jim Larkin, champion of the Dublin workers, and two months later a poem appeared in *Comhar* which is rather similar in theme to the McCaughey ballad. It is at first sight surprising that Behan should not think it more apt to honour Larkin in the language of the Dublin worker; a poem in Irish meant nothing to most of those with whom Behan had followed the coffin. The Larkin verses show how committed Behan was at the time to Irish. They are not particularly good, having the weaknesses of the previous effort without its strength. The structural looseness emphasises the lack of direction.

He was me—he was every mother's son of us,
Ourselves alone—strong as we wished to be,
    As we knew how to be.
He threatening fight and bringing freedom,
We following his coffin through the jaws of the city,
    Amid great bellows of rage.
Following his coffin through the jaws of the city last night,
Were we ourselves in the coffin?
No. We were marching in the street,
Alive—grateful to the dead one.

This is the assertion of emotion rather than the imaginative expression of emotion: there is no living sense of Larkin's greatness or of 'our' loss. As a socialist and an aspiring poet, Behan felt obliged to mark the occasion but the command performance lacks depth.

In 1947 Behan found himself in prison again for IRA activities. In Strangeways Jail, Manchester, it struck him that this was the same old story: that he would never achieve his literary ambitions but would be carried around the vicious circle of hope, political action, arrest and despair.[11] With a mail-bag needle he began to scratch out his troubled thoughts in a poem, 'Repentance'. This was a standard topic for Irish poets, and Behan wrote that the first stanza was a translation of an English verse which had come down from his maternal grandmother, but this poem as a whole achieves a life of its own and writhes with deep feeling. It is, in contrast with the earlier efforts, a private poem, unhindered by political abstractions. Far from being an assertion of emotions, the communication of the poem is in the expression, the sound, rhythm and syntax revealing the theme. The struggle between hope and despair, between faith in the Virgin and the masochistic orgy of self-accusation, emerges in the musical pattern of lingering supplicatory vowels and the harsh clamour of consonants and images of pursuit. The final stanza may be translated as follows:

> Recollection hoots like a hunting-horn
> Calling my sins like a ravenous pack;
> To the end of my trail comes death on a horse,
> Each year a jump behind his back;
> As I wait for the kill, cornered and panting,
> The bloodsweat breaking on my face,
> As I tremble before their red-eyed howling,
> Virgin, don't grudge me your merciful grace.

Here is a tone of voice which is rare in Behan's writings other than his Irish poems. Generally, in and out of his works, he projected himself as larger-than-life; the tough, cocky, jovial veneer covered more uncertainty than he cared to reveal and was, in biographical terms, self-defensive. In 'Repentance' and in many of the subsequent poems, the protective devices are dropped and it is possible to detect a direct honesty which is latent in his other works. The *persona* of the Irish poems would seem to be the closest approximation to his basic personality. Perhaps, because the language was so closely associated with his sense of literary vocation, writing in Irish enabled him to subject himself to confessional scrutiny; certainly, the monastic tenor of the life of the writer in Irish (especially when compared with the clamour of his public performances) allowed him to express himself with a minimum of self-consciousness. 'Repentance' describes the death-bed of a guilt-stricken sinner, but the temptation is strong to see the imagined death as a correlative of another doom which haunted him at the time—the death of the writer within him, dissipated in the aimlessness of his life.

He returned to Dublin but was unable to establish a productive routine: in 1948, after a bout of drinking, he ended up in Mount-joy. He recalled the vision he had had there six years previously: his lack of progress towards it worried him and inspired him to poetry. Superficially, the poem is an expression of nostalgia for life on the Blasket Islands; by 1948 almost all the inhabitants had removed to the mainland. Given what is known of Behan's atti-tude to the Blaskets and of his situation at the time of composition, the poem becomes more complex. The Blaskets were part of Seán Ó Briain's Gaelic Kerry, an ideal Ireland.

'I thought of the wonderful kind people [*the islanders*] were and the free and independent, if frugal lives they and their ancestors had on these islands, their eras of quiet happiness there on the uttermost fringe of Europe.'[12] The loss of the Blasket community was the loss of a symbol which he had hoped would help him integrate his political and cultural hopes. The islands had fallen, not to a foreign invader but to modern times. Similarly, the IRA had apparently been outmanoeuvred, not by an alien but by an Irish government. Was his hope of becoming an Irish writer to fail also? In such grey moments on the brink of despair he could imagine so. What was he but a Dublin house-painter imprisoned for drunken brawling?

The title, 'A Jackeen cries at the loss of the Blaskets', is interest-ing. 'Jackeen' is the non-Dubliner's term for the Dubliner: it is never intended as a compliment—implying as it does that the Dubliner has turned his back on his Irishness to ape English ways —yet Dubliners usually welcome it as a means of differentiating between themselves and others. There is an element of aggressive pride in Behan's usage here, in the idea of a 'jackeen' paying his respects in Irish. Behan's biographer rendered the title 'A Jackeen says goodbye to the Blaskets', and suggested that the poem was Behan's unconscious farewell to Irish poetry. This is possible but doubtful. 'Says goodbye' is not a good translation of 'ag caoineadh' in the context: it is final and resolved whereas the poem itself is full of fear and uncertainty and love.

> In the sun the ocean will lie like a glass,
> No human sign, no boat to pass,
> Only, at the world's end, the last
> Golden eagle over the lonely Blasket.
>
> Sunset, nightshadow spreading,
> The climbing moon through cold cloud stretching
> Her bare fingers down, descending
> On empty homes, crumbling, wretched.
>
> Silent, except for birds flying low
> Grateful to return once more;
> The soft wind swinging a half-door
> Of a fireless cottage, cold, wet, exposed.

This is a version of the nightmare which others have described as a waste land, a deserted village, a dark night of the soul: it is essentially an insight into Behan's own situation. The tears are not only for the islands but for all they meant to him. To take the conclusion as one of renunciation would be to over-emphasise the negative aspects and miss some of the complexity. The poem, dedicated to Seán Ó Briain, is an effort to hold on to something of value at a time when his life seems to be slipping away.

It was not long after this sentence in Mountjoy that he headed for Paris. Two lyrics date from this period. Behan was sometimes bought drink by people wishing to learn about Joyce's Dublin; he showed his gratitude in *Thanks to Joyce*, a casual *jeu d'esprit*.

> Here in Rue St Andre des Arts,
> In an Arab tavern, drunk,
> I explain you to an inquisitive Frenchman,
> Some ex-GIs and a Russian, drunk.
> I praise every single work of yours
> And as a result, in France, I drink liqueurs.
> You're the *conteur* we value the most
> And thanks, by the way, for the Calvados.
>
> If I was you
> And you were me,
> On the way from Les Halles

C

> With this load of cognac
> Full of grub and booze and glee
> You'd write a verse or two in praise of me.

The use of Irish in the context of cosmopolitan Paris complements the confidentiality of this grateful nudge. There were many such taverns in Paris and Behan's life developed into a series of sprees, but no amount of acting could disguise his frightened reaction to the house in which Oscar Wilde had died in 1900. He sought to exorcise the ghost by writing a poem. Short lines sketch the grim scene: once the prince of elegance, the scandal of high society, he now lies stretched out in a dingy Paris room, watched by guttering candles and a landlady who feels cheated of her rent. Towards the end, the immoralist had sought the consolation of the Church; Narcissus turned to holy water.

> Priestless death is risky
> Even for the happy sinner;
> More power to you, Oscar—
> Either way a winner.[13]

This finale tries to laugh away a poem which was no laughing matter: the image of an Irish writer reduced to a neglected 'foreign boozer' in the squalor of a cheap Paris room was not lost on Behan at the time.

All but one of his poems to date—the exception, if it is an exception, is 'Thanks to Joyce'—dealt with death. Those on McCaughey and Larkin avoided the physical fact by celebrating a metaphysical resurrection. In 'Repentance' the poet turned to heaven; in the case of Wilde, Behan escaped from the morbid spectacle by means of a humour which is slightly forced. Only in the Blasket verses is the vision presented and accepted without recourse to any comfort, but then the subject was not the death of a person but that of a community. Two other poems from 1949 are built on a triangle of love, life and death; though related in theme, they differ in tone and treatment.

'Grafton Street' is a night-poem, obscure in style and dark in intention. The obscurity is due to the distance between the poet's vantage-point and position of the people he is contemplating. The opening stanza establishes the hostility between them and their environment:

> Saw last night the living
> On death's island,
> Heard talk in a place
> Devoted to the silent.

In this same manner, rather like that of a hand-held camera, the next two stanzas focus on a girl. Details of her appearance—false shoulders, shampoo, Max Factor cosmetics—and her youthful laugh are set against the fact that she is tubercular. The fourth and final stanza tells how the pleasure of a brief physical love must be partially repressed, how even the doomed laughter must be muted:

> Whisper, as one must,
> Of love in this sour land
> Before they go in
> To dance in the Classic.

This little piece is Behan's most jaundiced vision of his native place and gives some idea of the difficulty he had in returning to live in Ireland in 1950.

The companion poem, 'To Bev' is a hymn to a girl who has feathered a comfortable nest for herself by smashing her way through the repressive atmosphere of 'this sour land'. In golden contrast to the dark night of Grafton Street, it exudes the sunshine of the countryside around Cahirdaniel, County Kerry, where it was written. Basically a *chanson* on the marriage of a rich old man to a lively young girl, it is also something of a parody of a traditional Irish form, the *aisling*. In the *aisling*, the poet encounters a beautiful female whom he assumes to be a goddess or a mythological heroine; she, however, tells him she is Ireland, longing for the arrival of her true lover (the Stuart Pretender) who will free her from the tyranny of the English king. Behan's apparition is not likely to be mistaken for Diana or Deirdre of the Sorrows, and if in the end she turns out to be Ireland, things have changed a great deal since independence.

> One sunny day I saw a vision,
> Her cloak, hat and dress the newest of new,
> In all respects elegant, expensive, in fashion,
> From the feather in her hat to the buckle on her shoe.

More pleasing than her dress was the laugh on her lips,
Her satisfied manner, the glint of her smile:
'True love my arse,' said she to me sweetly,
'I'd sooner my old man, my wardrobe and style.'

'I know nothing of scarcity, waiting or wanting;
I have all I desire and enjoy it in bliss.
If my husband is old, there's no end to his bounty
Lest he forfeit his conjugal right to my kiss.'

'My blessing on greed and intelligent marriage,
Bringing hundreds in banknotes and gold on request;
Utterly free from the sharp taste of shortage,
Of food and of drink I just order the best.'

The height of my joy is that no one will live
(Not the devil's own brother) to more than five score,
And so, in the meantime, what harm if the kitchen-
Window is open and a string hold the door?

How very different from the tightlipped gloom of 'Grafton Street'.

The Behan of sunny Cahirdaniel lingers in the public mind but the lines 'To Bev' come between two poems which are anything but lighthearted, 'Grafton Street' and 'Loneliness'.

The taste of blackberries
After rain
On top of the mountain
In the silence of prison
Cold whistle of the train.
The lovers' whispered laugh
To the lonely one.

In this impressionistic experiment, the paucity of disjunctive syntax allows the images to exist both in isolation and in various relationships to each other. One reading will suggest that the lonely person compares the bitter-sweet of the overheard laugh to the two earlier images of joy and isolation. Another will perhaps produce something like this: remembered confinement sweetens the blackberries, the sound of the train pains the prisoner all the more because it is travelling to where the blackberries grow, loneliness is worse for the person who has known love. The limpid melancholy seems to arise from the realisation that life has its Grafton Street as well as its Cahirdaniel.

In 1950 Behan wrote 'Guí an Rannaire' which was included in *Nuabhéarsaíocht* along with the Blasket verses. 'Guí an Rannaire' is, in the context of this study, the most interesting of his poems. The precise connotations of the title are important. It is doubtful if there is any current English equivalent of 'rannaire' which is less pejorative than its usual rendering 'versifier'. A 'rannaire' is (in this case) a writer of verse who is not a poet or 'file'. (The early modern English 'rimer' was very close in meaning.) The distinction may seem over-fine, but this is because English lacks some word to differentiate between the poetical practitioner and the poet. History is not so broadminded : precedent would suggest that of the legions of poets writing today, only one or two will continue to be considered poets in a few decades.

> If some grown-up guy, with fluent Irish,
> Wrote of people and things in a civilised style,
> Of moods and opinions in the words of today,
> Impudent, easy, expansive, *au fait*—
> I'd happily hear what he had to say.
> A poet with punch, with power and plenty,
> A burgeoning bard, blazing and brazen,
> Pained, impassioned, paganpenned.
>
> But Jesus wept! what's to be seen?
> Civil servants come up from Dún Chaoin,
> More gobdaws down from Donegal
> And from Galway bogs—the worst of all,
> The Dublin Gaels with their golden *fáinnes*,
> Tea-totalling toddlers, turgid and torpid,
> Maudlin maidens, morbid and mortal,
> Each one of them careful, catholic, cautious.
>
> If a poet came and inspired some spirit,
> I'd go home, my job finished.

It is difficult to envisage a translation doing full justice to sound and sense. The gusto, the concatenations and the apt choice of key-consonants recall Merriman's *Midnight Court*, a legal saga of the battle between the love-hungry women and the repressed men of Ireland. Merriman's work was frowned on by some, but it circulated in manuscripts. Seán Ó Briain had a copy in Mountjoy and it was probably by means of this that Behan acquired something of Merriman's comic rhetoric. Later on he translated *The Midnight Court* into English and included the opening lines in *Borstal Boy*; it is said that he translated all one thousand lines of the work but lost the manuscript in a punch-up.[14] Merriman does not use alliteration as a merely metrical device; he chooses and varies the key-consonants—ebullient plosives, sneering sibilants, vituperative fricatives and so on—to reinforce the narrative without ever becoming excessive. It is not difficult to imagine the appeal of his poem for a prisoner-student: it played physical deprivation against sensual abandon and surveyed love, lust, greed, marriage and the clergy with a verve which even today retains a *risqué* excitement. Behan's effort, another broadside against the prim and proper, resurrects Merriman's verbal power.

'Guí an Rannaire'—the prayer of the 'rannaire'—is aimed at the hyper-respectable element in the national movement, epitomised by the shrewd rustic who makes good in Dublin, where his knowledge of Irish is useful for state employment. The twin emblems of this group are the pioneer-pin, denoting their pledge to abstain from alcohol, and the *fáinne*, a ring worn on the lapel by those willing to converse in Irish. Brought up in a repressive form of Catholicism as puritan idealists, they are attracted to organisations of national renewal, including the IRA. As an intense and religious child, Behan had become involved with such people but he grew up to detest their bourgeois piousness. His own knowledge of the Gaelic tradition told him that such narrowmindedness was a recent innovation: the poets, even those who took the precaution of writing a *repentance*, were generally a wild lot. Behan resented the image of Gaelic Ireland which was held up by the language-enthusiasts of 1950. As a poet, he was in the forefront of the battle for revival, yet among those who shared this hope he found nothing else in common. His poem is really a prayer, an ejaculation in time of sore temptation to give up, a prayer to Mother Ireland that this chalice might pass from him. Yet he will hope and hold on awhile.

Within this framework, another drama is enacted. Behan is not being falsely modest when he describes himself as a 'rannaire' rather than as a 'file'. He feels that he is not the great poet capable of igniting the ashes of Irish society; if such a poet were to come on the scene, Behan would withdraw, having carried out his rear-guard action. He lists the qualities which this messianic figure would need: a modern mature mind, capable of poetry which was passionate and radically exciting. Behan himself wrote very little poetry after 1950, but not because the 'file' had come. Towards the end of 1950 he began to create *Borstal Boy*, the main theme of which was the development of a modern Irish mind. It was both an account of his time in England and a compressed history of his life to date. In a less obvious way it was a history of Ireland in his own time. Was this the work to which the 'rannaire' had looked?

> . . . of people and things in a civilised style,
> Of moods and opinions in the words of today,
> Impudent, easy, expansive, *au fait* . . .

The novel was not in Irish, but it was in the language of Ireland. Behan had injected his poetry with the modernity of Dublin and Paris but it is unlikely that he could have written a sustained work in Irish which was up to the standards laid down by the 'rannaire'.

> . . . with punch, with power and plenty,
> . . . burgeoning . . . blazing and brazen,
> Pained, impassioned, paganpenned.

This energy appeared not in his poetry but in *Borstal Boy*.

'The Coming of Spring' was published in October 1951. It is a poem of wintering out: the poet prepares for the hardships of winter in confident expectation of a new year's growth. The title and the reference to St Brigid's Day recall Raftery's poem, but Behan's is more introverted and private. The taut lapidary style of the short Irish lyrics suits Behan's intentions better than Raftery's *amhrán*.[15]

> Harsh Irish winter
> I loathe your face
> The north wind comes
> Strong shaken pained
> No growth or good
> No lift or life
> Till bright St Brigid's Day
> And joy's revival.

> Comes the south wind
> Pledge of sun for my frame
> Exciting new life
> The blood awakening.
> Winter weather
> Old men's time
> Welcome and thousands
> Spring of youth.

He had come back to Ireland to labour on his novel; the confidence of the working writer is reflected in the formal economy of the poem, in the tight lines and unstrained flow.

One more poem remains. 'L'Existentialisme' is really a verse doodle, but is not without its own curious interest. Subtitled 'An Echo of St Germaine-de-Prés', the poem presents replies as ironic echoes of questions.

> Watchman, walking the wall—
> of an empty hall.
> What is the chase after?
> a grave matter.
> A journey to hell?
> Of course, but your mind as well?
> What was before our time?
> Dunno. I wasn't alive,
> amn't yet.
> Evil our fate?
> too lazy
> to say.
> Virtue, not a gleaning,
> nor pain, nor even meaning,
> nor truth in what I posit—
> nor in the opposite.

As a doodle, it succeeds in vanishing up its own question mark with a yawn; as a comment on the fashionable cult of existentialism, it is mildly amusing. Why write it in Irish? It has no apparent connection with Ireland. If the original impulse was satirical, would it not have been better served by parody which came so easily to him in English? What inspired the piece?

The watchman or sentry is on guard but it is possible that he is wasting his time. His assiduity on the wall is mocked by the sinister, dismissive antiphon:

of an empty building.

This is repeated, less specifically:

What is the course of the hunt?
a matter of the grave.

If all endeavour leads to the grave, is all effort futile? The interplay of endeavour and futility is not resolved and this seems due more to the poet's lassitude than to his existentialist principles. Huge abstractions are introduced and, too tired to ponder them, he allows them to drift away into careless negation. It would be dangerous to read too much into such a lightweight piece, but if this is, as it seems to be, Behan's last attempt at Irish verse, there is probably some relationship between the sentry and the *rannaire* of the rearguard. (There was an Old IRA periodical called *An Fear Faire*, the term Behan uses for sentry or watchman.) The *rannaire* knew that he was holding the fort only until relief came. Was he wasting his time? Was the hope of an Irish revival a hollow one? When dealing with Behan's poetry it is often useful to look at the poem in the light of his attitude to the language. 'L'Existentialisme', which opens with a suspicion of futility and fades away into vacuity, may well have arisen from a crisis of faith similar to that which inspired the *rannaire*—loss of confidence in the future of Irish and in his own ability as a poet. If so, it marks also the loss of that military resolve to remain at his post until replaced.[16]

4

The Quare Fellow

> I have been in the theatre business all my life, for one section of my family have been supplying costumes, running theatres and owning cinemas for generations. From the age of four, I had watched good old melodrama at the Queen's Theatre in Dublin . . .[1]

Shortly after his arrival in Mountjoy Jail in 1942, Behan was known as a cheerful extrovert with a talent for storytelling and an ambition to write.[2] He was working on a play, *The Landlady*, based on the most extravagant character of his childhood, his Granny English. His cousin Seamus de Burca, himself a playwright, made a typed copy of the play—a hundred quarto pages, double-spaced—and offered advice. As he saw it, *The Landlady* was a 'slice of life' but there was not enough action to sustain the play. The dialogue was sound, the structure a series of tableaux. The principal happening was intrusively melodramatic: a young girl, pregnant and rejected by the Landlady's son, attempted on-stage suicide with an open razor.[3] An Irish audience of the day would have reacted strongly against a slice of Irish life which included illicit sexuality, attempted suicide, a prostitute with an illegitimate child and the muted suggestion of an incestuous relationship between the Landlady and her son. Behan must have been aware of this and, presumably, part of his intention was to shock people. In this respect at least he succeeded: an attempted production in Mountjoy was prevented by some irate prisoners who supported their criticism with physical violence.[4]

Ulick O'Connor commented on the qualities of the dialogue which *The Landlady* shared with the works of Sean O'Casey: Behan, he claimed, was not copying O'Casey but was 'reproducing the same world that O'Casey did'.[5] It is true that both of them were using the same raw material, but surely Behan was imitating O'Casey or, at the very least, being strongly influenced by him. It is difficult to see how a Dublin working-class dramatist of the forties could avoid the shadow of O'Casey and his three early plays of tenement life. Behan had been brought up to be proud of the famous dramatists Ireland had produced—Sheridan, Wilde, Shaw—and as he grew older he must have been especially pleased to add O'Casey's name to the list. The others, because Anglo-Irish, were not people with whom Behan could identify, no matter how much he admired them. O'Casey, though born a Protestant, was almost a neighbour: brought up in poverty in a northside tenement, self-educated, involved with the left wing of the separatist movement, disenchanted with the results of Ireland's independence. O'Casey combined his literary with his political career: he was a committed writer whose radicalism had offended the cultural elite in Ireland; he alone of the early Abbey dramatists wrote, not of ancient heroes or rural peasants, but of the slum-dwellers of Dublin. His life, his works and, not least, his success made him an inspiration for the young prisoner-playwright.

In the early forties in Ireland, O'Casey's fame rested almost entirely on his three early plays *The Shadow of a Gunman, Juno and the Paycock* and *The Plough and the Stars*, and on his row with the Abbey over *The Silver Tassie*. These plays were populated with a range of characters, most of whom would have been familiar types to Behan, and the dialogue was activated by a dramatic language based on the Dublin dialect which Behan used himself in his public performances. There was another reason why Behan should find these plays congenial examples. O'Casey's perception of the fight for Irish freedom was rather similar to that at which Behan was arriving: that while the issues involved were nationalism and imperialism, the ordinary poor had nothing to gain and a great deal to suffer in the cross-fire.

Behan was willing to concede that *The Landlady* had its faults, but he defended the characterisation and, by implication, the dialogue. The characters were based on real people, he wrote in a letter:

I don't mean to say that any of them are exactly and in every detail as I described them (and I painted them, didn't photograph them). But I do claim to have taken nine real Dublin slummies and stuck them on paper. I even go so far as to claim that they are as genuine as any of O'Casey's battalion—maybe more so, because O'Casey was born a Protestant and that seems a big lot.

It is not immediately clear in what way they are perhaps more genuine. Behan's claim was probably based on the fact that his dialogue is closer to the actual speech of the people and has not been exaggerated or stylised in the manner of O'Casey. The letter continues:

> No, I don't think the faults of the piece lie there. I've a good idea of them and the principal one is that altho' one section of my family were then and are, immersed in the theatre, I myself never went to a play except to be entertained. . . . Therefore I know little of the art of stagecraft and, until I had the idea of writing plays, cared less.[6]

The letter makes clear that Behan had come to acknowledge the technical flaws which Seamus de Burca had pointed out but it also implies that, if he could master this aspect of the art, he could at least emulate the early O'Casey.

There are differences between *The Landlady* and the work of O'Casey other than those of construction. Rather surprisingly at first sight, Behan avoids the political element: perhaps this was because the world of his Granny English was for him non-political, but it was more probably due to his unwillingness to show himself as being less orthodox than his action in Liverpool and Glasnevin would have led his fellow-prisoners to believe. As has already been suggested, his language is less edited than O'Casey's, which is very often a highly contrived variation on the vocabulary and rhythms of Dublin speech:

> . . . an' any kid, livin' or dead, that Jinnie Gogan's had since, was got between th' bordhers of th' Ten Commandments! . . . An' that's more than some o' you can say that are kep' from th' dhread o' desthruction be a few drowsy virtues, that th' first whisper of temptation lulls into a sleep, that'll know one sin from another only on th' day of their last anointin', an' that use th' innocent light o' th' shinin' stars to dip into th' sins of a night's diversion!

This extract from the second act of *The Plough and the Stars* is not to be confused with the actual speech of a tenement woman. From what remains of Behan's play it is clear that he has taken less licence with the everyday speech of the people, although the reference to Job in the following extract probably owes more to O'Casey than to the dialect of Russell Street:

> That's what I said to the priest too, and he said that Job, the lad in the Bible went through great difficulties too and came through them, with his flag flying. 'Well, Father,' says I, 'but was Job's daughter left with a bellyful of disgrace by a dirty animal like Mickser Moran, was she Father.' 'Oh' sez he, 'These little crosses are a sign of God's favour' 'Well, Father,' sez I, 'even if they are signs of favour, I'd sooner have no more of the same signs.'[7]

The introduction of Job is managed successfully and humorously: he gets over the problem of his difficult daughter as well as any Dublin lad. Otherwise, there is no element in the speech which one might not hear even today in parts of Dublin, but Behan, like O'Casey, has allowed the colourful elements to accumulate with a prodigality one does not find in everyday speech.

In prison, especially when the planned production of the play was scrapped, Behan had little chance to acquire the technical skill which was needed to improve *The Landlady*. However, a new stimulus caused him to work on the play again. As has been shown in a previous chapter, Behan was one of those prisoners influenced by a resurgence of interest in Irish writing in the forties. Translation would seem to be an obvious first step towards writing in a second language and he chose to translate *The Landlady*. It was, in many ways, a strange decision. The manager of the Abbey, Earnán de Blaghd, was a fervent supporter of the Irish language and was bound to look favourably on a new Irish play. On the other hand, he was anything but a liberal either in politics—he had been a hardline member of the Free State government—or in literature. Even in Irish, *The Landlady* would probably strike him as offensively immoral. From a letter he wrote to de Blaghd in May 1946, it would seem that Behan had begun reworking *The Landlady* in English while beginning another play in Irish, and that he then discovered they were both essentially the same play and merged them in a new Irish version of *The Landlady*. (Unfortunately, de Blaghd's rejection is lost.) The latter part of

Behan's letter is even more interesting: 'I have written one Act of another play. *The Twisting of Another Rope* I call it, because everything is shown in the *black cell* in some prison. Two men are condemned to death and waiting for the Rope—I would send it with this but better not scare the Department of Justice before we have anything done. There is nothing political in it, of course.'[8] This is the first reference to what would later become *The Quare Fellow*. In this version, written in Irish in 1946, at least some of the action took place within the condemned cell and presumably the doomed man was present on the stage; in the final version in English, many years and drafts later, one never sees the 'quare fellow' or his cell.

In Mountjoy, Behan had met two men who were condemned to death by hanging, one for butchering his brother, the other for drowning his wife. (It is said that Behan saved the latter's life by jeering him so much that he was declared insane and sent to an asylum.[9]) Bernard Kirwan, who dissected his brother, was a strange person who embraced Behan the day before his death and promised that he would pray for him in heaven. Few people could easily forget such a kiss, least of all Behan who was aware how horrifyingly close his own offence had brought him to execution.[10] Later on in Mountjoy, Behan lived through another execution and on this occasion the circumstances were even more disturbing: the victim was a young man who had fired a shot at the police— a charge on which Behan himself had been found guilty.[11] On the eve of the execution he must have recalled his agony in Walton Jail in 1940 when the IRA men, Barnes and McCormack, were hanged in Birmingham for their alleged part in causing explosions in Coventry. There again he had been tormented by the knowledge that he had come to England to plant bombs, that it could so easily have been his neck in the noose.[12] Is it any wonder that death figures so prominently in his writings? The play which was set in *the black cell* was entitled *Casadh Súgáin Eile (The Twisting of Another Rope)*. 'Casadh an tSúgáin' *(The Twisting of the Rope)*, is a beautiful love-song which tells how the lover was deprived of his girl: her parents invited him to make a rope in her house and, when he moved his chair out the doorway, they locked him out. The theme of the song does not seem to be particularly relevant to Behan's play but the title was. Douglas

Hyde had dramatised the story and this little one-acter is normally considered the first play of the Irish-language theatre; Behan, perhaps unconsciously, hoped that his play would be the first of a revived Irish theatre. One also suspects that the emphasis on the *other* rope indicates his awareness of the rope which was to be used, not on Barnes or McCormack or Kirwan, but on the spectre which haunted Behan—his imagined self who had not escaped.

Casadh Súgáin Eile was rejected by the Abbey but the raw material was too much a part of Behan to be forgotten. Shortly after his release from the Curragh it came to the surface again. In January 1947 he attended a meeting of IRA men who were planning a concert in commemoration of the deaths of Barnes and McCormack. When it was suggested that the programme should include a one-act play on the subject of the 1798 Insurrection, Behan argued that what was needed was a play about Barnes and McCormack and, when it was pointed out that no such play existed, promised to provide one himself within forty-eight hours, which he did. The play was entitled *Gretna Green* and showed three people outside a prison on the eve of a double execution; it would be clear to anybody at such a concert that the prison was Winson Green and that the two to be executed were Barnes and McCormack. No copy of the play survives but those involved recall that there was little action and that the impact of the play was hindered by the freezing cold weather which left the organisers with a half-empty house.[13]

When Behan promised a play in two days, he clearly had some idea of what it would be like. His confidence must have been based on his work on *Casadh Súgáin Eile* and on his awareness of the part played by Barnes and McCormack in the complex of feelings which had found expression in a play about the hanging of Bernard Kirwan. The fact that he himself had not been in the prison where they died led him (if he had not done so previously) to set the scene outside *the black cell* so that the victims and the execution exist only in the minds and words of the chorus without —a device which was to shape *The Quare Fellow*.

Although Behan was happy that his play had had a production, he was not content to leave it at that. He persisted with the play as set in Mountjoy on the eve of the Kirwan hanging. When working for Radio Éireann in the early fifties, he hoped that it would be broadcast. He showed Francis MacManus a draft of a one-act entitled *The Twisting of Another Rope* but it must have been a fairly rough draft for MacManus remembered it as 'a few pages of a play about a man who was condemned to death for boiling his brother.' Having made no impression on Radio Éireann, Behan turned yet again to the Abbey where de Blaghd advised him to develop it into a full-length play. When Behan had done this, de Blaghd suggested that Behan might go over the play with an Abbey producer to see if it could be made shorter and more suitable for staging; de Blaghd was also worried that some official in Mountjoy would consider the play actionable. Behan, reacting to what he felt to be a superfluity of advice, undertook to revise the play himself but it was the same script he sent back to the Abbey and it was rejected.[14] The play did the rounds of the theatres in Dublin, unsuccessfully until it fell into the hands of Alan Simpson and Carolyn Swift who had recently converted an old coach-house into a theatre, the Pike.

Behan found the Pike much more congenial than the Abbey: the play was accepted on condition that he made some revisions and he did so willingly, even to the extent of changing the title of which he was so fond into the much more striking *The Quare Fellow*, the name given by the prisoners to the condemned man.[15] The Pike production was excellent and the play very well received, yet none of the larger Dublin theatres was willing to take it over when offered. Though it was an unqualified success, the Pike production actually lost money because of the large cast and the tiny capacity of the converted coach-house. However, *The Quare Fellow* had far to go. In 1956 Joan Littlewood put it on at the Theatre Workshop in London and after a three months run and critical acclaim it moved to the West End.

Whether they like it or not, the people who come to see *The Quare Fellow* take an important part. There is a short interval of darkness between the switching off of the auditorium lights and the rise of the curtain during which is heard a resigned voice singing a melancholy song. When the curtain rises, the audience sees a prison landing. 'On the wall and facing the audience is printed in large block shaded Victorian lettering the word "SILENCE".' (1)[16] This is as much a test of the audience as an instruction to the prisoners. The audience is examining an institution which it has created, sanctioned and maintained itself. The audience is society: it must respect its own security system, must certainly not laugh at it. The audience may seek to escape its role by claiming that it knows nothing of prisons and allows them to be run by experts. Behan's play makes them expert in at least one field of penology, hanging.

> The man that feels it worst, going into that little house with the red door and the silver painted gates at the bottom of D. Wing, is the man that has been in the nick before, when some other merchant was topped; or he's heard screws or old lags in the bag shop or at exercise talking about it. A new chap that's never done anything but murder, and that only once, is usually a respectable man, such as this Silver-top here. He knows nothing about it, except the few lines that he'd see in the papers. 'Condemned man entered the hang-house at seven fifty-nine. At eight three the doctor pronounced life extinct.' (7)

An indication of the power of the play is the manner in which it alters the audience from the respectable 'new chap' to the experienced lag. After *The Quare Fellow* it is impossible to see judicial hanging as an element in an argument on crime and punishment: Behan has infixed in our minds the physicality of the action and the actuality of the hours before it.

Though we never see it, the hang-house has a *red* door and the gates are painted *silver*. The operation which takes place inside is as lively as the paintwork. The dynamics of hanging are complicated, relating the weight of the body to the length of the drop, allowing for variations in the dimension and texture of the neck. (79f.) It is beyond the scope of pure science and indeed it demands the personal attention and intuitive eye of the craftsman: 'He says he can judge better with the eye. If he gave him too much one way he'd strangle him instead of breaking his neck, and too much the other way he'd pull the head clean off his shoulders.' (65) Every care is taken to ensure the success of the victim in his next life: in the case of a Catholic, the hood is slit and socks taken off immediately to facilitate anointing. (81) A young Protestant clergyman showed himself guilty of weak faith while attending one of his persuasion to the gallows: although he saw the washer being correctly placed under the victim's ear he was unable to watch the hanging body and fainted. (63) Nor is it only during the actual hanging that the welfare of the subject is taken into account. His last hours on earth are filled with luxuries which are the envy of other prisoners—special food and more cigarettes than he can smoke. The warders are strictly instructed to prevent any depression. 'An air of cheerful decorum is indicated, as a readiness to play such games as draughts, ludo, or snakes and ladders; a readiness to enter into conversation on sporting topics will also be appreciated.' (66) Regulations also stipulate that nobody is supposed to know the right time.

Despite the elaborate machinery, some are not impressed, especially those with long experience of prisons.

> In the first place the doctor has his back turned after the trap goes down, and doesn't turn and face it until the screw has caught the rope and stopped it wriggling. Then they go out and lock up the shop and have their breakfast and don't come back for an hour. Then they cut your man down and the doctor slits the back of his neck to see if the bones are broken. Who's to know what happens in the hour your man is swinging there, maybe wriggling to himself in the pit.

It is reported that one man lived for seventeen minutes at the end of the rope. (8) A prisoner who had actually seen a body after hanging would not like to do so again: 'his head was all twisted and his face black, but the two eyes were the worst; like a rabbit's; it was fear that had done it.' (22) The audience may not be inclined to believe the testimony of prisoners, some of it based on rumour, but it is corroborated by one of the warders:

> And you're not going to give me that stuff about just shoving over the lever and bob's your uncle. You forget the times the fellow gets caught and has to be kicked off the edge of the trap hole. You never heard the warders below swinging on his legs the better to break his neck, or jumping on his back when the drop was too short. (76)

This is disturbing and the person of the executioner does not help to exorcise the spectre of such inhuman bungling. He is drunk and, despite his apparent know-how, his total lack of any feeling for his subject is frightening. And who is to say that he has made a mess?

It has been objected that the play 'lacks the unifying focus of a central character'.[17] Surely the central character is, as the title suggests, 'the quare fellow' himself. He is to be hanged and the theme of the play is the effect which his fate has on the people within the prison and, by the extension already mentioned, on the audience. The dialogue is seldom far removed from 'the quare fellow'. He does not appear on the stage but this does not prevent him from dominating it in the minds of others. We do not know his name or anything personal about him: all we know is his crime and his punishment. A great deal of the dramatic tension in the play arises from this. The prison system has devised a procedure whereby the condemned man is kept apart. One wonders why. Can it be that they who are about to kill him are acting in his interest? Is it not more likely that they are trying to keep the business as quiet and as secret as possible? That they feel that there is something shameful, something obscene, in the idea of legal execution? And is this why the prisoners and staff refuse to mention the victim by any personal name? The 'quare fellow' is taboo: all attempts to hide him and to dehumanise him are attempts to disguise the fact that he is a human being who is about to be killed in a careful calculated manner. The audience does not see him; all society ever sees is 'the few lines in the papers'.

Yet everybody knows he is there in the little house with the red door and the silver painted gates, that the warders bring him attractive meals and so many cigarettes that his throat is parched, that the hangman will peep in at him and note the strength of his neck, that he will be taken out in the morning and be left dangling at the end of a rope until dead. The dramatist does not allow us to *see* him on the stage despite the fact that he is the principal participant in the action. The audience should not be surprised: society, that is they themselves, ordains that a similar technique be used in real life.

The Quare Fellow is a play within a play, and structurally much more sophisticated than it is often thought.[18] There are two audiences: those in the theatre watch those on the stage who witness the externals of the closet-drama. Those on the stage react in various ways to the ritual in which they play or are forced to play some part. Some of them, prisoners mostly, seem to be callously unconcerned with the fate of the unknown victim; others, most of the people who are part of the system, accept the procedure as sanctioned by religion, morality and social necessity. The theatre-audience cannot resist judging the behaviour of those on stage and invariably they laugh at the black humour of the prisoners and dissociate themselves from the strict principles of the prison regime. At some point during or after the play the theatre-audience must realise that they have been tricked into a position which is critical of the very institution which they support outside the theatre.

The audience does not discover the judge who sentenced the victim in their name nor the minister who chose not to reprieve him. Our representative on stage is the Governor. A responsible man, he is shocked to hear that one of his warders made a joke about the execution. He himself was acutely embarrassed at his School Union where he was subjected to some tasteless remarks about the hanging: some young pup asked him to sing 'The Night before Larry was Stretched'. He will have it known 'that there's at least one place in this city where an execution is taken very seriously indeed' and that is in the prison which he commands. (74f.) The term 'seriously' seems suspect in one who is more upset by the threat to his dignity at the School Union than by the duty of stage-managing an actual death. As a rule, the warders are not an attractive lot: they are self-seeking, sly and quick to ingratiate themselves with their superiors by criticising their colleagues. Their fixation with 'pay, promotion and pension' is not unduly disturbed by the execution. (51, 68ff.)

The exception to the rule is Regan, the most articulate commentator on the action. The character closest to the audience, Regan's reactions are those of the average, reasonable human being. For the same reason, presumably, he is the only official who earns anything like affection or respect from the prisoners. His colleagues suspect him, seeing in his emotional confusion a threat to the professional discipline which makes their work acceptable. Regan has difficulty in reconciling his religious beliefs with the use of capital punishment. The representative of the Department of Justice concludes that Regan's Catholicism is not quite that defined by Rome; one of the prisoners concludes that Regan must be an atheist. (56)[19] When asked why he remains a warder, Regan replies with characteristic sarcasm that 'it's a soft job, sir, between hangings'. (33)

Regan offers much more than sarcasm: his analysis of judicial hanging disturbs both his colleagues and the audience because it uncovers physical facts which *the system* is at pains to conceal.

It is Regan who insists that everybody takes part in the hanging. To the official from the Department who, while favouring the system, does not see that he has any part in it, Regan insists that the job is ours: 'Yes, ours, sir. Mine, the Canon's, the hangman's, and if you don't mind my saying so, yours, sir.' (32) Not only does he refuse to use the professional hangman as a scapegoat, he also rejects the antiseptic jargon: his job is 'neck breaking and throttling'. He savagely counters the point that the condemned man is given an opportunity to die a holy death and gain eternal life:

> We can't advertise 'Commit a murder and die a happy death,' sir. We'd have them all at it. They take religion very seriously in this country. (29)

Regan's problem is that he cannot see how 'the law makes this man's death someway different, not like anyone else's'. (75) His ability to continue his role in what he considers an obscene charade almost breaks down just before the arrival of the hangman. When urged by the Chief to keep his curious ideas to himself, Regan, according to the stage direction, *almost shouts*:

> I think the whole show should be put on in Croke Park; after all, it's at the public expense and they let it go on. They should have something more for their money than a bit of paper stuck up on the gate. (76)

The image should not be lost on the theatre-audience. Manic hilarity suggests a mind at the end of its tether. Regan's humour is not facetious; it is a final desperate defence-mechanism and, because we are given a deeper insight into his character than into that of the others, it should help us to understand the grim humour of the prisoners.

During the first two acts, the theatre-audience is offered two versions of the fate which awaits the 'quare fellow', the neat and civilised *coup de grace* supported by the system, and the crude strangulation proposed by the prisoners and Warder Regan. Society has decided that the prisoners are unfit company for us; the prison staff express strong doubts as to Regan's character. It is just possible that what attracts the audience to Regan is his human weakness rather than his knowledge of penology, that his frightening vision of legal execution as a circus of unrealised potential is the product of a disturbed mind and a slander on the system. What finally convinces us that Regan is right is the arrival of the hangman in the third act. The professional and socially sanctioned terminator is hardly what was expected. An habitual drunkard, he enters drunk, bawling out a sentimental love-song, accompanied by a hymn-singing assistant. The hangman is jovially sociable and insists that Regan have a drink with him: he sees himself as everybody's friend, a popular landlord of a pub in England, a religious man. He once got out of his sick bed to hang a soldier and would 'go a 'undred miles to do a man a good turn'. (78) He claims that the hymns of Christian mercy which his assistant sings bring tears to his eyes but when the assistant sings, the hangman works out the equation which will solve the 'quare fellow'. (The sight of him making his calculations while drunk revives the stories of bungling on the gallows.) What is most striking about the hangman is his total unawareness of his victim as anything other than a prop in his routine; his humanity has been buried beneath familiarity and the sedatives of alcohol and religion. He is, by any standards, insane. He would be delighted if Regan's nightmare came true, if the execution were presented as public entertainment: he sees himself as the Ringmaster of the Circus. (74)

On the title-page, *The Quare Fellow* is described as 'a comedy-drama'. It contains elements of both tragedy and comedy but, lacking the eventual defeat of the darker forces, it is not a tragi-comedy, in the accepted sense. In theme and effect, the play is closer to tragedy but some such term as comic-tragedy or black comedy seems more apt a description. The characteristic mark of the play is its treatment of a terrible event in a manner which provokes laughter. It is possible to distinguish between the component parts which excite different kinds of laughter in the theatre. The Governor, for example, provokes satirical laughter: the audience thus expresses its disapproval of his heartless concern with the appearances of order in such a situation. The same is probably true of the hangman: the audience despises his moral and emotional myopia. The effect of Regan's sarcastic suggestion that the 'show' be put on in a football stadium is different: here the audience laughs not out of a sense of moral superiority but in grateful relief. By pushing the real threat of horror into the realm of surrealism, Regan has disarmed it for the moment, both for himself and for us.

Most of the humour in the play is aroused by the prisoners. Initially it seems that they are brutally insensitive, emotionally calloused by experience. They do not know why one prisoner was reprieved and not both but suspect that the decision was based on aesthetic or social grounds:

Well, I suppose they looked at it, he [Silver-top] only killed her and left it at that. He didn't cut the corpse up afterwards with a butcher's knife . . . Yes, and then of course the other fellow used a meat-chopper. Real bog-man act. Nearly as bad as a shotgun, or getting the weed-killer mixed up in the stir- about. But a man with a silver-topped cane, that's a man that's a cut above meat-choppers whichever way you look at it . . . So as to be on the safe side, and not to be making fish of one and flesh of the other, they usually top both. Then, of course, the Minister might have said that enough is as good as a feast. (4f.)

The prisoners never question the victim's guilt nor the right of society to punish. They have their own standards of crime and punishment: they see little difference between them and, in the above quotation, describe both in culinary terms. They speak a language of their own, replacing the clinical jargon of penology with a jocular argot: hanging is 'topping' or 'a haircut and shave', the victim is 'the quare fellow'.

Dunlavin is the senior member of the convict community. He has spent most of his life in jail but unlike most others who have done so 'he has not become absolutely dulled from imprisonment'. (3) He is at home in prison: for him, as for Neighbour, outside freedom is nothing to look forward to.

Neighbour: Only then to wake up on some lobby and the hard floorboards under you, and a lump of hard filth for your pillow, and the cold and the drink shaking you, wishing it was morning for the market pubs to open, where if you had the price of a drink you could sit in the warm anyway. Except, God look down on you, if it was Sunday.

Dunlavin: Ah, there's the agony. No pub open, but the bells battering your bared nerves and all you could do with the cold and the sickness was to lean over on your side and wish that God would call you. (23)

Dunlavin's life is dedicated towards a basic survival. He loathes the man from the Department and the smug morality he epitomises, yet Dunlavin polishes his chamber-pot in order to win his good will. Dunlavin knows that he is selfish but sees this as a necessary tactic in his battle against 'the cold of the wind and the world's neglectment'. (27) His strict ethical code makes no exceptions for condemned men. He gets a smoke for the reprieved prisoner but reminds him: 'But remember the next wife you kill and you're getting forty fags a day in the condemned cell, think of them as is not so fortunate as yourself and leave a few dog-ends around the exercise yard after you.' (15) Dunlavin is obviously not as hard as he pretends. He expresses his disgust at having a sexual offender near him: 'You wouldn't mind old Silver-top. Killing your wife is a natural class of a thing could happen to the best of us. But this other dirty animal on me left . . .'(5) He later relents: 'Ah, when all is said and done, he's someone's rearing after all, he could be worse, he could be a screw or an official from the Department.' (26) He would, even then, recognise human nature, albeit in its lowest forms.

Dunlavin has survived because he has learned to pick little holes in the system and to accept his lot as best he can. What has prevented him from becoming 'absolutely dulled' is his sense of humour. He consistently provokes our laughter and most of the time we laugh with him rather than at him, as he petitions the sanctimonious Healy or cajoles Regan. In order to get at methylated spirits he tells Regan that his left leg pains; when Regan points out that he has put his right leg out, Dunlavin replies:

> That's what I was saying, sir. The left is worst one day, and the right is bad the next. To be on the safe side you'd have to do the two of them.

If Dunlavin's logic is dubious, his humour is irresistible:

> It's only the mercy of God I'm not a centipede, sir, with the weather that's in it. (26)

His gift for comic description is seen at its best in his lectures on the serious business of law and order, crime and punishment. While the condemned prisoner is pampered but is not allowed to know the time, Dunlavin transposes the scene in the cell into farce. The warders will not tell the time.

But they put a good face on it, and one says 'There's that old watch stopped again' and he says to the other screw 'Have you your watch, Jack?' and the other fellow makes a great joke of it, 'I'll have to run up as far as the North City Pawn shop and ask them to let me have a look at it.' And then the door is unlocked and everyone sweats blood, and they come in and ask your man to stand up a minute, that's if he's able, while they read him something: 'I am instructed to inform you that the Minister has, he hasn't, he has, he hasn't recommended to the President, that . . .' (6)

Black, but nevertheless farce. Gradually, the audience realises that Dunlavin and the other joking prisoners are not being callous or sadistic: they are using the only means at their disposal to ward off the horror that they know only too well. So great is their physical comprehension of approaching death that they must fight against it in order to preserve their sanity. They will do anything rather than face the facts. They will joke about it, they will bet on it and they will try to make a profit on it, but they will not face it. They will try to live out the normal prison life as if nothing unusual were about to happen. They will try to disguise the humanity they share with the victim by refusing to give him the individuality of a name, by expelling him from themselves to the land of the unknown as 'your man' or 'the quare fellow'. For as long as possible they will use a crude form of word-magic to banish the primitive fear which they feel within themselves.

The climax of the play comes in the first part of the last scene. The warders in the prison yard count the minutes, seven, six, five. The process of time is hidden from the victim; the prisoners, knowing that time has defeated their defence-mechanisms, make one last desperate attempt to deny death. Five minutes before the execution is due to take place, the hush of the yard is broken by a loud voice imitating (this would be clear only to an Irish audience) a well known sports commentator, Mícheál Ó hEithir. The voice is that of one of the prisoners: he does not actually see the hanging but describes it vividly as a horse race.

We're off, in this order: the Governor, the Chief, two screws Regan and Crimmin, the quare fellow between them, two more screws and three runners from across the Channel, getting well in front, now the Canon. He's making a big effort for the last two furlongs. He's got the white pudding bag on his head, just a short distance to go. He's in. [*A clock begins to chime the hour. Each quarter sounds louder.*] His feet to the chalk line. He'll be pinioned, his feet together. The bag will be pulled down over his face. The screws come off the trap and steady him. Himself goes to the lever and . . .

It is difficult to resist the mad humour, especially when the motivation is appreciated. It recalls Regan's attempt to disguise the killing by proposing that it be staged as a public entertainment in Croke Park, the stadium from which Mícheál Ó hEithir often made radio commentaries. Even the almost insensate hangman sought some relief by imagining the business as a circus turn. The characters use such black humour in an effort to exorcise the spirit of death. The manic hilarity is an eruption of a primitive life-drive, a last stand which testifies not only to the prisoners' fear of death but also to their basic sympathy with 'the quare fellow'. Hence their reaction:

> *The hour strikes. The* WARDERS *cross themselves and put on their caps. From the* PRISONERS *comes a ferocious howling.* (83f.)

Escapism and exorcism have failed: abandoning all verbal pretence, the prisoners howl like wounded animals. Meanwhile the warders salute the authorities, religious and secular, which sanction their participation.

The play does not end on this high note of climax. The remainder of the scene shows the recuperative powers of the prisoners and the system. Neighbour's delight at having won Dunlavin's bacon in a bet is frustrated: Dunlavin announces cheerfully that he has been put on a milk diet. The moment of identification with the victim was shortlived. His grave should be marked E.779 but it is decided that E.777 is much easier to carve. Regan had intended that the victim's letters should be buried with him but the prisoners realise their value and, in a business-like manner, arrange to share them in an equitable way and sell them to one of the Sunday papers. The play closes with a prisoner's musical fantasy of what life would be like in the female prison.

The Quare Fellow is a compelling play, from the first apparently tasteless joke to the final graveside obscenities. It is impelled by the humour of the prisoners and is, literally, desperately funny until it sheds all defensive articulation in the 'ferocious howling' of the climax. Some of the compulsive power is due to the role, that of society, which the audience is forced to play. The dramatist ensures that, during the play, society will identify with the insecurity of the prisoners rather than with the moral certainty of the staff. The audience is judge and jury but finds itself in the strange position of showing gross contempt of court by frequent laughter.

The play has been criticised as 'a rather shallow bit of propaganda directed largely towards the evils of capital punishment'.[20] To deny this is not to deny that Behan was opposed to capital punishment or to underestimate the assistance the London production got from a contemporary campaign against hanging, but the play itself is not essentially propagandist. Regan is the only character who offers anything like explicit criticism of the system and even he fails to offer any active resistance. The prisoners, because they are aware of its crudeness, criticise it on physical grounds but accept it as an aspect of a social order which they find inherently hostile. The Governor and his staff know that they are merely carrying out the instructions of society. Thus there is nothing of the tract in the play and it retains its impact even where capital punishment has been suspended. Its effect should be felt wherever there is an imperfect society which, in its desire to organise itself for the good of the majority, makes imperfect laws which alienate the exceptions, the unusual, the 'quare' fellows. (It is not necessary to believe in the burial rites of ancient Greece in order to be moved by Sophocles' *Antigone*.) Though the play is an occasion of laughter it is by no means shallow, for the laughter springs from the darkest depths of our consciousness and registers the rebellious vitality of man against the forces of oppression, dehumanisation and death.

To its credit, the play lacks the simplicity of propaganda. There is no sentimental utopianism and no attempt to show man as greater or less than we know him to be. The audience laughs at the Governor not because his comfortably small mind is alien to us but because it recognises the Governor in itself, and this holds for the other characters, including the hangman.

The play is structurally sound and is, perhaps, the only work by Behan of which this may be said. Nothing is superfluous: those elements which are not immediately concerned with the central action—for example, Dunlavin's methylated spirits and the prisoners' admiration of the females in the laundry yard—not only serve to establish the penal atmosphere but also show the efforts of the prisoners to preserve some semblance of normal life. The anticlimax which follows the hanging underlines other aspects of the horror by showing the lack of respect for the victim even in death: staff and prisoners are eager to forget what has happened and to get on with the business of life. Once again, the relationship between the characters and the audience is hinted at: the audience will soon leave the theatre and go back to their normal lives. Both audience and characters have attended a play, an imaginative version of what actually happens, although neither has seen it. The dramatist controls the reactions of the characters in order to direct the reactions of the audience. Far from being thematically unsubtle or structurally unsound, it is dramatically extremely effective and a deeply moving play. The persistence of the theme in Behan's mind and the strange structure of the play—the unnamed victim, the imagined agony, the drunken camaraderie of Death the Entertainer and the hysterical climax—suggest that the dramatist was attempting to exorcise some horrible recurring nightmare of his own, the twisting of another rope, another neck.

5

Borstal Boy

In December 1943 Brendan Behan wrote from Arbour Hill Jail
to a republican friend, Bob Bradshaw:

> Then of course since I was sixteen (all but a few months) I've
> been in jails and Borstal Institutions. I don't regret my time in
> England. (IRA prisoners in Ireland I've discovered are an un-
> interesting and boring lot.) It provided me with material for a
> book on Borstal which I'll get fixed up after the war and with
> material for numberless short stories, one of which *Borstal Day*
> you may borrow from Sean . . . I had some other stuff I'd
> like you to have seen. Some short stories about the '39 cam-
> paign and the beginning of a long novel I'm doing on it, title
> *The Green Invaders*. Traynor, Adams, etc, have apparently
> accepted me as a sort of official historian of it and it's with their
> assistance I'm doing it. (I mean in the line of verifying facts,
> etc—the impressions noted and conclusions drawn will of course
> be mine.)[1]

The letter is invaluable because of the information it contains not
only on Behan's writings but also on his rather confused state of
mind. It is hardly the sort of letter one would expect from the
IRA Volunteer who had invaded England single-handed and who
had fired at the police at Glasnevin and who had, as he points
out, spent practically all his adult life in confinement as a result.
There is no sign of the political extremism which excited those
actions nor any element of bitterness against his enemies. Even
stranger is the implication that he found his term in England,
alone in a hostile environment, more interesting than his present
sentence during which he is enjoying the privileged status of a
political prisoner among his republican comrades. He is assessing
his experiences not as a member of the IRA but as a writer: he

looks forward to his release not in order to recommence his political activities but to get down to writing 'a book on Borstal'.

It would be a mistake to take the letter too literally and to assume that by the end of 1943 he had revoked his allegiance to the IRA. He did not, in fact, find all his fellow-prisoners boring and, within a few months of release, he would serve another sentence in an English prison for IRA activities.[2] At the time of writing to Bradshaw he was irritated by something and used his IRA comrades as scapegoats. The something was almost certainly his failure to resolve to his own satisfaction his twin roles of writer and political revolutionary. To a great extent, his dilemma is illustrated by the fact that he mentions two books, both dealing with the 1939 bombing campaign. The IRA officers have more or less commissioned him to lend his literary talent to the cause by writing 'a sort of official' history of the campaign. The arrangement is by no means clear. Presumably Behan's superiors want a factual account which is sympathetic to the IRA, yet Behan insists that he will be in overall control, and refers to the work (which he has begun) as a 'novel'. The plural of the title, *The Green Invaders*, suggests that it would feature all those who had been active in England. Was this an opportunity to rewrite his own efforts and those of his Granny Furlong into the official annals? How would he combine first-hand experience with objective research? With hindsight it is obvious that the entire project was misconceived: Behan's literary talent was not the sort to satisfy the requirements of a serious political organisation. Even the title was weak: opponents of the IRA would take 'green' to indicate not only the nationality of the participants but also their lack of expertise. When the leadership accepted Behan 'as a sort of official historian', they were unaware of any incongruity and this may have been what irritated Behan who knew that he was the person in the world least suited to the task.

More than most, he knew what was expected of the literary republican: he had been reared on the writings of men like Tone, Mitchel and Clarke, men whose accounts of their sufferings for Ireland served as primary texts for successive generations of rebels. When Behan was arrested in Liverpool, he was proud to point out how Tom Clarke had been captured in much the same manner.[3] For his involvement in the Fenian campaign in England towards the end of the nineteenth century, Clarke had been sentenced to penal servitude for life but was released after fifteen years. On his return to Ireland he became one of the prime movers in the events which led to the 1916 rebellion and was executed shortly afterwards. His book, originally serialised in a republican periodical, is a harrowing description of a penal system which was apparently designed to drive men to insanity. Clarke made no claims to literary talent: he wrote to show how far Britain was willing to go in order to suppress Irish republicanism and how much Irish republicans must be prepared to endure. He never accepted that he was a criminal or that he had anything in common with the non-political prisoners—a standard republican position—and he left prison more convinced than ever of the necessity to continue the struggle against the British.

Behan had followed in Clarke's footsteps and had endured the special treatment which British warders reserved for Irish incendiaries, but that was the extent of the resemblance between Clarke's case and his own. If Behan had served fifteen years in Walton Jail he might have been brutalised by torture into an undying hatred of all things British. In fact, he spent only four months there and maintained a sense of perspective.

The trial of Barnes and McCormack was proceeding and therefore I understood the bitter cruelty of my captors, even to a boy of sixteen. The uniformed police at Cheapside were swine, the warders at Walton Prison were worse, my fellow-prisoners were as bad as either (under official direction). From this condemnation I exempt the plain clothes CID who actually arrested me, the Church of England chaplain who said 'good morning (?)' to me. I especially remember the insultingly brutal behaviour of the Roman Catholic chaplain and the prison doctor.

These remarks are contained in an unpublished manuscript which was probably written shortly after his return to Ireland, perhaps in Mountjoy.[4] The memory of Walton was still painfully fresh, so much so that Behan was unwilling to continue with the 'chronicle of torture' which his account of Walton constituted.

From Walton, after his trial, he was taken to Feltham Boys' Prison where youths were interviewed in order to discover to which Borstal they were suited. Behan praised the liberal thinking behind the system.

Not that any of the officers knew anything about the thinking that had built the system, but as the ordinary simple person is decent enough when let be, they applied it as efficiently as they'd apply the most repressive statutory (?) rules and standing orders in an ordinary prison.

Behan became friendly with one warder, a former British Army engineer with whom he discussed military engineering. This warder almost killed Behan with kindness, providing him with enormous numbers of potatoes which Behan, out of decency and gratitude rather than appetite, ate. The manuscript begins to describe 'the only difference I had in Feltham with anybody', which concerned the celebration of St Patrick's Day, but Behan drops the subject and crosses out what he had written on it. Shortly afterwards Behan was transferred to Hollesley Bay, designed for 'the younger lads (16-20) with sufficient sense of responsibility to live in an open Borstal'.

Although we were handcuffed to a long chain with an officer either end of it, I'm sure the people on the road took us for holidaymakers, for every conceivable song was sung in the ninety miles from Feltham to Hollesley Bay. I sang Irish popular songs and Borstal songs and many of them Irish ballads that had drifted in thru' the British Army—'Kevin Barry' and what can be regarded as the national anthem of the social underground of these islands 'MacCafferty' . . .

It is obvious that, far from holding himself aloof from the 'common' criminals, Behan rejoiced in their company and was accepted as one of them. Just how far he deviated from the traditional republican position is made clear from the following account:

If we'd had girls in Hollesley Bay I'd have applied to spend the rest of my life there. Nowhere else have I met an almost classless society. Nowhere was I loved so well, or respected so highly. I've my letters home to prove that I thought that at that time too. I loved Borstal boys and they loved me. But the absence of girls made it that much imperfect. Homosexuality (of our sort) is not a substitute for normal sex. It's a different thing, rather similar to that of which T. E. Lawrence writes in *The Seven Pillars*. The youth of healthy muscle and slim-wrought form is not the same as the powdered pansy (who I hasten to add, as good as anybody else, has every right to be that and a bloody good artist or anything he wants to be). Our lads saw themselves as beautiful and had to do something about it. About a third of them did. Another third, not so influential or less good looking, would have liked to. As I say however, without women it could not be a pattern of life, only a prolonging of adolescence—it was as beautiful as that.[5]

This was surely the book which Behan wanted to write, a story not of political defiance but one of survival and development by means of friendship. He must have known that he could not take up such a subject in prison, where even *The Landlady* had raised the passions of some of his colleagues. These same people would regard his friendship in Borstal as fraternising with the enemy, the element of homosexuality as an obscene insult to the good name of republicanism. The 'book on Borstal' would have to be postponed till he found some privacy when released. Meanwhile he could treat some of the *safe* material in short stories and tinker with the 'sort of official' history of the campaign which would maintain his reputation as both republican and man of letters.

Shortly after Behan's arrival in Mountjoy, the Governor had arranged a visit by Sean O'Faolain. The immediate result of this meeting was that the June number of *The Bell* carried a story by Behan entitled 'I Become a Borstal Boy', an account of his experiences in Walton Jail on 7 February 1940. On that day, by a coincidence which Behan never forgot, Barnes and McCormack were executed for their alleged part in the Coventry explosion and Behan himself was tried and sentenced to three years' Borstal detention. Though the story shows promise its chief interest lies in its being the first surviving attempt at what would become *Borstal Boy*. A comparison between the story and the novel is informative.

There are two conflicting styles or tones in the story. The first, dominating the opening section, is neutral.

I awoke on the morning of the 7th February, 1940, with a feeling of despondency. I'd had a restless night and fell asleep only to be awakened an hour later by the bell that roused myself and 1,253 prisoners in Walton Jail.

D

As I awoke the thought that had lain heavily with me through the night realised itself into words—'If they carry it out'. Just then I heard the shout 'Right, all doors open. Slop out.' They will die in two and a quarter hours.

Later on, the narrator (whose name is Brendan) is told by 'a Monaghan lad of Republican ideas and many convictions' that 'they' have died. Brendan leads a demonstration in the prison chapel, calling the Irishmen to attention: 'We will recite the *De Profundis* for the repose of the souls of our countrymen who gave their lives for Ireland this morning in Birmingham Jail.' The warders use violence to break up the demonstration but just as the narrator is about to be hit, the Principal Officer orders him to be spared because he is due in court that day. The reader is not told who the dead Irishmen are or why they were executed. He suspects that they were found guilty of IRA activities and that Brendan Behan is the leader of the IRA prisoners in Walton Jail.

In section two, one discovers that Brendan Behan is a cocky sixteen-year-old, quick to answer the teasing warders. On the way to court in a small police car he finds himself with a Mr Crippen who is on trial for murder: 'I was wondering in what form to put my own question, for it seemed rude to ask "Who did you kill?" At last I found a more delicate formula. "Who was the deceased concerned with your case?"' Suspicions of Behan's republican affiliations are confirmed when he recognises the names of IRA men scratched on the wall of the cell and inscribes a quotation from Pearse. The more exuberant tone which emerged in the dialogue of the second section takes over completely in the third which describes his trial.

Amid a fanfare of trumpets the judge entered and seated himself. Then the clerk, magnificently arrayed in what appeared to be a red hunting jacket, began the list of alleged offences that constituted the bone of contention between the King and myself.

Behan refuses to plead but, when found guilty of unspecified crimes, he accepts an invitation to speak.

I proceeded to speak and he [the judge] interrupted me and told me that what I was saying wasn't likely to induce him to give me a light sentence. However, I had learned the speech off by heart and thought it rather good and I did not intend to be sentenced without getting the worth of my money, so I told him that if it was all the same to him I would prefer to continue.

The 'rather good' speech is not recorded. The judge feels that the maximum sentence for a juvenile is inadequate in the circumstances but can only send Behan down for three years' Borstal. Behan, having said goodbye to Crippen (who is taken to the condemned cell) estimates the probable date of his own release and settles down to sleep.

Readers of *Borstal Boy* can see what Behan is trying (and failing) to do in 'I Become a Borstal Boy': to describe his emotional turmoil in Walton Jail on the day Barnes and McCormack were executed. Their deaths brought home to him the fate he might so easily have met himself. He admired them but the harsh realities of Walton Jail had tempered his desire to share their martyrdom. He wished to preserve his loyalty to the ideals he shared with them but, most of all, he wanted to survive. This he had managed to do, not because of any immutable adherence to political principles, but by adapting himself to his new circumstances. Writing in Mountjoy in 1942, he was, for reasons already suggested, unwilling or, perhaps, unable to resolve the contradictions of his position. Hence the inconsistencies of the story, the failure to assimilate the two voices which would form the dramatic synthesis of *Borstal Boy*, where the executions in Birmingham serve to illustrate the conflict within the narrator. In the *Bell* story, it is difficult to believe that Behan is genuinely shaken by the events in Birmingham even though he risks the warders' wrath in order to demonstrate his solidarity: he is no sooner out of the chapel but he is admiring his own felicity of diction and enjoying himself at the expense of the court. The story is also weakened by the witholding of the crucial information which links the narrator with the men in Birmingham.[6]

As we have seen, Behan abandoned his 'book on Borstal' and hoped to resume it on his release. He wrote a good deal during the remainder of his sentence but nothing, as far as can be judged, immediately related to *Borstal Boy*. When, shortly after leaving the Curragh, he began again, he faced what seem like his earlier difficulties. He sent *The Bell* an account of the IRA camp where he had trained before crossing to England; it was rejected 'on the grounds that his treatment of the subject . . . did justice neither to himself nor to the people mentioned in the article.'[7] The editor at the time, Peadar O'Donnell, a radical republican who had written a minor classic of prison literature, *The Gates Flew Open*, was neither narrowminded nor unsympathetic to Behan himself; one presumes, therefore, that the treatment of the instructors and trainees must have been totally lacking in seriousness and respect in order to place it beyond the bounds of O'Donnell's appreciation. The voice which had emerged triumphant from the conflict of the earlier story was not that of the staunch young man who had led the demonstration but that of the cocky teenager with a preference for the comic.

In the summer of 1947 Behan was in prison in Manchester, for activities connected with the IRA. In an interview he gave many years later, he associated a crucial change of direction with this sentence: 'I stopped trying to find political solutions and began seriously to write.'[8] It was hardly the first time he made this resolution—in the letter to Bradshaw he expressed the intention 'to put a curb on my [conscience] when I get out'—but the evidence suggests that he was more in earnest on this occasion.[9] As a freelance writer it was inevitable that he should tap his experiences of prison and the IRA. With the editor of *Comhar* he discussed an Irish version of his penal memoirs and later wrote a series of articles for *Comhar* on the bombing campaign. The articles were possibly based on what he had written of *The Green Invaders*. The approach is far from disrespectful: he wrote that, being the youngest, he was the 'pet' of the training camp and the only hint of friction appears in a reference to the Camp Commandant: 'We did not get on too well together because I did not fancy the *Let-me-carry-your-cross-for-Ireland* line to which he was given.'[10] Generally speaking, Behan's analysis of the campaign is, from the IRA's point of view, orthodox.

Late in 1952, he found himself in prison yet again, this time in Sussex, for illegally entering Britain on his way to France to write an article commissioned by the *Irish Times*. During his stay, he read extracts from a novel to a fellow-prisoner.

Although I had written an article about Borstal which was published in *The Bell* ten years before, I spent most of my time extending it, so that when the week got well under way I had more or less completed the rough draft of a book. This was later to appear as *Borstal Boy*, but I re-wrote it several times before the final version was published.[11]

This gives the impression that, during this sentence, he expanded the original story into a version of the novel; in fact, 'most of my time' must be taken to refer to the period between 1942 and 1952. In May 1951 he wrote in a letter that he 'had started a book' called *Borstal Boy*; in the following year he reported that he had 'about 50,000 words done'.[12] (This would comprise a draft of about half the size of the final product.) He had hoped that his friend, John Ryan, would publish sections of his work in progress, but they came too late for *Envoy* which ceased publication in 1951. (*Points* accepted *Bridewell Revisited* and published a slightly modified version of it in the Winter 1951 issue.) The archives of *Envoy*, acquired by the Morris Library of Southern Illinois University in the late sixties contained three typescripts of *Borstal Boy* material.[13] They show clearly the evolution of the book.

The shortest of these is entitled *Deliverance* and is an account of Behan's feelings immediately prior to his transfer from Walton to Feltham Boys' Prison. It is the 'chronicle of torture' from which he had recoiled when writing *The Courteous Borstal*. The mood is one of seething hatred, the style an interior rhapsody based on a liturgical litany. The piece is dominated by the opening word 'deliverance' which is followed by sketches of the prison staff, the Chief Warder, the Governor, the doctor, the priest, the parson and the Principal Officer.

Deliverance—

From the Chief Warder. Squat over-washed ex-terror of the foc'sle and chief arse licker to the quarter-deck.

'Good type this Hunt, stern disciplinarian, don't know how we'd get on without him. Make a splendid—railway detective, labour spy, night-watchman, game-keeper, bank messenger.'

'Half a crown for your trouble, my man.'

'Thank you, sir, glad to be of service, sir.'

'Black and Tan. Palestine Policeman, clean as a whistle, clean and clammy as a cod, faithful employee.'

'Robert, when you take over, remember Hunt. He's given very loyal service. Particularly good at weeding out undesirable

types. Remember him, let not poor Hunty starve.' Prison
service, good opening for right man, Chief Warder, Chief
Bully of the wretched, the broken, the young.

This embittered fantasy is much more savage than the jovial abuse
which a more resilient Behan poured on the regime in *Borstal Boy*.
It exudes a naked hatred which is missing in the novel. He later
left a very unpleasant picture of the Catholic chaplain in the novel
but in *Deliverance* Fr Lane is transformed into a black litany of
all that is evil in imprisonment.

From the priest. Big belly Lane.
'Dearly beloved, and Saint Paul teaches us that the greatest
of these is charity. Our Divine Lord shows us the great example
of love—love as wide as the farthest horizon, as deep as the
deepest ocean—You there at the back, remember that you're in
the House of God, you irreverent blackguard. Mister, take that
man inside and lock him up. Bring him before the Governor
in the morning. He's been talking during the whole service.
Even during the litany—
'Cause of our Sorrow,
Discomforter of the Afflicted,
Gate of the Hanghouse,
Tower of Granite,
Bars of Steel,
Frightener of the Sick,
Bully of the Young,
Persecutor of the Aged,
Breath of Booze,
Palm of Pederast,
Sustainer of Stranglers,
Torturer of the Timid,
Darkness of the Day,
Scream in the Night.'

There is no equivalent of *Deliverance* in the novel, where Behan
and his mates are 'in great humour . . . though . . . a bit im-
patient' during the last days at Walton. *Deliverance* is a powerful
passage and Behan must have found it hard to leave it out of the
novel. He probably reasoned that the satirical style—based on pure
hatred and tending to dehumanise those described—did not fit

into the final version of *Borstal Boy* where the perspective is invariably more humorous and humane.

The two other pieces from the *Envoy* archives reappear in *Borstal Boy* in revised form. One deals with the Callan-episode, looking back to 'I Become a Borstal Boy' and forward to pages 132-142 of the novel. The character of the narrator has changed considerably since his first uneasy appearance in *The Bell*. He is no longer the leader of the demonstration nor even a willing participant:

> When they executed the two others at Birmingham Callan had kicked up a fearful row. He was a mad Republican, and counted himself one of us, although he got his eighteen months for pinching an overcoat from Max Miller the music hall comedian. In two months Walton Jail had made me very anxious for a truce with the British. I'd have given them another six counties to be left alone. But Callan was mad and afraid of nobody.

Behan admits that if he were at home in Ireland he would 'roar proud defiance of the foe'; but his position in Walton makes him more circumspect. The night before the execution, Callan roars anti-British slogans and calls on Behan to join in. Behan is caught between loyalty to the cause and fear of the consequences: mentally cursing Callan, he makes some timid noises in Irish. He continues till he hears Callan being beaten unconscious by the warders. Asked by a warder what he is doing at the ventilator, he replies:

'I'm saying my prayers, sir.'

There are several minor alterations in the novel—Callan's praise of Hitler, Behan's use of Irish and his lie about praying are dropped—but the essence remains. However, the version in the novel is amplified and undeniably improved. The story of Callan's ventriloquism in the exercise yard—where he causes the prisoners to march about as if they were at an IRA rally and provides the bagpipe-music himself—is brilliantly told; the quotations from *Cranford* (the book is merely mentioned in the typescript) capture perfectly the frightened prisoner's dream of distant domestic bliss.

It would be impossible to fault Behan's revision of the Callan-episode; his reworking of the other typescript, *Bridewell Revisited*, has been censured.[14] *Bridewell Revisited* covers the first eighteen pages of the novel, Behan's arrest and first day of captivity. The later alterations come under three headings: minor changes of phraseology, a softening down of swear-words and 'bad' language, and the radical rewriting of three episodes. As regards the first two, there is no real problem. The minor changes are made to make the narrative move more fluently and are generally success-ful; the language was toned down in accordance with current publication standards. The thinking behind the other revisions is less immediately obvious and more interesting.

The first concerns the statement Behan made at CID HQ. The typescript reads: 'I agreed to make a statement, with a view to propaganda, for the Republic. Ultimately, I suppose, for myself. Revolutionary politics are forms of acting. Ghandi ne'er cast a clout, nor Goering ne'er turned a jowl camerawards with more care than I took with that statement.' The actual statement is more or less as in the novel but the afterthought is very different: 'The God save Ireland was an extra bit of hypocrisy, intended for the Dublin papers, for the people at home who would be reading them.' The cynicism is that of a mature adult reviewing—with some distaste—the posturing of his youth. What emerges in the later version is the voice, not of an objective adult, but of a teen-ager, sufficiently emotional to have taken the risk of crossing to England and to be slightly shaken by his arrest. He believes in his vision of himself. By including the reference to the reaction in Dublin, the novelist allows the reader to smile, but the hero is excluded from this creative conspiracy because he is too busy see-ing himself among his great predecessors in the fight for Irish freedom. From the beginning the typescript grants him self-knowledge; the novel will describe his gradual progress towards it.[15]

Between the writing of *Bridewell Revisited* and the final draft-ing of *Borstal Boy*, the author decided to write from the inside, to re-enact the experiences rather than recall them. For this pur-pose he created a *persona* whose perception was very different from his own at the time of writing. The changes made in the book resulted from such a decision. He was right to emend the early account of the prisoner masturbating:

Oh, Cathlin Ni Houlihaun, your way is a thorny way. Much you knew about it, Yeats, yourself and Maud Gonne, bent over a turf fire reading Ronsard.

A horny way, you mean. Wonder if Emmet did it in prison, or de Valera? Who'd have thought the old man had so much blood in him?

And, tingling all over, pleasantly tired from the exercise, I fell asleep.

This is very clever stuff but the reader is following, not the activity of a forlorn prisoner, but the scurrilous agility of the writer as he skips from *The Shadow of a Gunman* to *Macbeth* by way of a veiled scholarly allusion to Yeats and references to Irish history past and present. Such university-type wit and the conjunction of Emmet with de Valera are not in character with the *persona* of the novel.[16] This episode is not used in *Borstal Boy* to raise a guffaw, but to underline the prisoner's unease as he suspects his physical inability to sustain the ideals which had formerly directed him.[17] His later conception of *Borstal Boy* also led him to cut what is possibly the most moving part of *Bridewell Revisited*. Behan's temper rises when abused by a warder who expresses the hope that Behan will be hanged. He knows how to strike back—by reminding the warder that German bombs will soon leave Liverpool a heap of cinders—but he realises that this form of retaliation would seem to place him on the side of the fascists against whom many Irishmen fought in Spain. He recites their names in an effort to control himself, but it is in vain. After his broadside he is filled with regret.

I thought of Ernst Toller and of the demonstration I marched in when I was twelve, because they would not let him enter Ireland. And I allowed that stupid old swine of a turnkey to rile me into betraying himself. Into applauding Toller's jailers, the murderers, the killers of his swallows.

It is not out of character that the prisoner should be aware of the Spanish Civil War; nor is it unlikely that he should have taken part in a left wing march before his arrest—he later claimed to have written for socialist periodicals before coming to England.[18] His crisis of conscience is not out of character; it is out of place, coming too soon in the story. The conflict with the warder shows Behan the futility of a political theory based on nationalism: theoretically, he should now support the English who are at war with Nazi Germany. In the context of the novel, this is too intellectual and too neat. Behan's idea was to trace the slow development of the prisoner's consciousness, not intellectually but emotionally, to use his experiences of people and places rather than abstract argument. Even towards the end of the novel, Behan is unable to offer any articulate resistance when his fellow-painter urges him to look on their Borstal colleagues as 'a dirty degenerate lot of scum'. Typically, Behan *feels* that they are not, but is unable to prove it to his mate.[19] It was necessary therefore to excise the extract from *Bridewell Revisited* which gave the prisoner an insight into his position (in the opening pages of the novel) much clearer than that which he would have at the end of his sentence.

Even without the typescripts, it would be possible to show that *Borstal Boy* is not autobiographical in the sense of a faithful account of Behan's imprisonment in England, but the revisions are invaluable as a means of discovering Behan's eventual intentions. *Borstal Boy* is an imaginative autobiography: Behan uses his experiences as the basis for a novel—just as Joyce did in the *Portrait*. The theme of the novel would be Behan's survival and psychological development; he would treat his material in a selective manner, moulding the actuality to suit the theme.

He worked assiduously on the book through the early fifties. His confidence and his application were encouraged with the Dublin production of *The Quare Fellow*, his marriage in 1955 and the establishment of his international reputation which followed the success of *The Quare Fellow* in London the following year. He sold extracts from his novel to English newspapers in 1956 and, early in 1957, had been approached by a representative of the London publisher, Hutchinson.[20] Behan accepted a £350 advance and promised to finish the book as quickly as possible. Shortly afterwards, he and his wife arrived in London with 'three hundred pages of foolscap', but not only was the book unfinished but Behan was loth to part with the manuscript. It was not until late in September 1957 that the publisher managed to badger Behan into supplying the outstanding hundred pages of typescript.

His behaviour prior to the publication of *Borstal Boy* is difficult to understand. Here was the opportunity he had awaited so long, the reward for fifteen years' labour and struggle against considerable odds; yet now he hesitated, delaying the whole process, refusing to supply the finished manuscript until forced to. Why?

He was, it is true, basking in the success of his play, but this does not account for his apparent lack of industry: in March 1957 he undertook to write a play in Irish for the tiny Dublin theatre run by Gael Linn. His hesitation had unfortunate consequences. It has already been shown how shrewdly and how masterfully he edited the early drafts to fit his later idea of the novel. In the summer of 1957 he lost that sense of control. The final section of *Borstal Boy* is loose and he should have been able to see that and correct it. It is in many ways an anticlimax, failing to sustain the pitch of the first two sections and weakened by several repetitions and passages of flaccid writing.[21] What had happened to the ambitious professional?

The probable answer lies in a remark he made in his publisher's office in the spring of 1957. Behan was more interested in clowning than in discussing his book. When the editorial director of the firm persisted and asked how much of the work remained to be done, there was a 'note of irritation' in Behan's dismissive reply: 'It's all lies,' he said.[22] The tone recalls something of the dilemma which he had faced when he contemplated the novel in Mountjoy Jail, surrounded by fellow-members of the IRA. He had been asked to write *The Green Invaders*, the historical account of the 1939 campaign, but had instead written a comic novel. In the meantime, Behan had drifted away from the IRA, deciding that his task was not to find political solutions but 'to mirror what happens to the people involved'.[23] It was not difficult to maintain this position during the early fifties. The IRA itself had barely survived the forties but had managed to reorganise sufficiently to launch an offensive campaign against Northern Ireland in December 1956. A few weeks before Behan discussed the publication of *Borstal Boy* with the Hutchinson representative, two young men, Sean South and Fergal O'Hanlon, were killed in an attack on Brookeborough Barracks. There were enormous displays of emotional sympathy throughout the country and the two men were soon the heroes of popular ballads. Predictably, the Dublin government cracked down on the IRA and reintroduced internment in the Curragh. In the circumstances, Behan's resolution to confine himself to writing was severely tested. Even if he was not actively involved in the resurgence of the IRA, many of his friends were; although the initial explosion of support for the IRA faded with the end of the campaign in the summer, the military action reminded those who might have forgotten that the IRA was still dedicated to the cause of a free and reunited Ireland. While Behan was enjoying himself in the literary pubs of London, he knew that, back in Ireland, old comrades were suffering for beliefs which Behan had once shared with them. If Behan did not give intellectual support to the recent IRA campaign, he was emotionally attracted to the objectives and to many participants. At the very least, it was to him a serious and complex matter; yet he knew that some members of the IRA would resent his comic treatment of his own involvement in *Borstal Boy*. Publishing the novel was clear proof of his decision to be a writer and not a soldier. The events of 1957 gave him pause but did not stop him. However, when people in London praised the book to the skies, Behan felt obliged to dismiss it as 'lies'. It was his way of telling 'the old enemy' that his book was not to be taken as political history.

Borstal Boy is a true history, not of a political campaign but of a single participant. A comparison with Thucydides' *Peloponnesian War* clarifies the scope of Behan's novel. Thucydides had also taken part in a campaign which he later chronicled. Given that he was not a disinterested onlooker, his account is as free from personal bias as one can imagine. (Thucydides had been censured for his military inefficiency; the reader depends on editorial notes to discover that this Thucydides is none other than the historian.) The Athenian was not primarily interested in individuals or individual actions: he tried to disclose the underlying pattern, the historical process which was expressed by generals and armies much as a dramatic text was performed by actors. He did so, not because he was particularly fatalistic but because he felt that the war, in its deep causes and strange logic, was too enormous to be comprehended from within. Thucydides the Athenian soldier was supressed; Thucydides the poet-historian took over. He gathered and arranged his material with a touch so light as to seem effortlessly and translucently objective.

Thucydides wrote in the belief that the war between Athens and Sparta was of great significance and that he himself had played a minor part in it. Behan believed that the 1939 bombing campaign was important *because* he had been involved in it. He came to see that it would hardly merit a footnote in the history of twentieth-century Europe, that it would soon be forgotten by all except those interested in the IRA; yet, simultaneously, he discovered that his involvement—almost non-existent from the military point of view—was the major event of his life. It had changed his vision of existence and made him what he was; from the personal point of view, his time in England was more important than the Spanish Civil War, the entire campaign in England and the Second World War all together. Style being the attitude of the artist to his material, Thucydides' urbane prose is the perfect medium for his history. Behan's experience demanded something radically different, the individual style of *Borstal Boy*. If Thucydides' mode is impersonal and translucent, Behan's is emotional and prismatic: everything is subjected to the refraction of the narrator's personality. Rather than describe the events from a remove of time and place, he gives the impression that he is reliving them, taking the reader into the mind of the prisoner. He does not allow any distinction between the narrative style and the quoted conversation of the character, Brendan Behan. Consequently, an atmosphere of a spontaneous delivery is created. Behan was a gifted 'live' performer, spellbinding audiences with a chain of stories and songs, but it would be a mistake to assume that the transcription to the printed page was an easy one: beneath the apparent spontaneity there is a considerable literary technique.[24]

The 'live' entertainer or storyteller has at his disposal the resources of mime and voice-inflexion; the novelist is limited to the immobile printed word and must compensate by varying pitch and rhythm. Behan's decision to fix the narrative focus within the mind of a young Dubliner led to another problem. The youngster is intelligent but he is emotionally confused and unable to point his own development in intellectual terms. The omniscient narrator may direct his reader by inserting elucidatory comment but Behan chose not to use this convention. He had to realise and control the inner drama while confining himself to the *persona* of a teenager. He resolved his difficulty by allowing the development of the youngster's mind to emerge through his changing reactions to his environment, implying these changes by subtle transformations in the narrative style.

The book opens abruptly with the arrival of the raiding detectives. Neither the room nor the detectives are described in much detail. In place of description we are given Behan's imaginative appraisal of his situation. Surprisingly enough, he is not utterly dejected: he rejoices in the possibility that the house will be damaged by the mob outside.

> This landlady was mean and as barren as a bog. Her broken windows would be a judgement on her for the cheap sausages and margarine she poisoned her table with, for she was only generous with things which cost little in cash, locking hall doors at night time and kneeling down to say the Rosary with the lodger and her sister, who always added three Hail Marys for holy purity and the protection of her person and modesty, so that you would think half the men in Liverpool were running after her, panting for a lick of her big buck teeth. (12)[25]

The absent inhabitants loom larger than the detectives, but here again there is no attempt at realistic portraiture: one finds instead an impressionistic gouache of cheap food, repressive piousness, steaming lechery and protruding teeth. The gusto of the satire derives from a combination of strong detail, surrealistic treatment and rhetorical delivery which will be a feature of the book. The staid rules of English syntax are abandoned after the opening statement of meanness and barrenness: these two ideas are then developed with fervent speed as clause follows clause with only commas dividing them until the realities of the lodging-house reach a surrealistic crescendo which involves half the adult male population of Liverpool in libidinous riot. The movement comes to a sudden stop on those 'big buck teeth'. Nothing more is heard of the house or its occupants but the passage has introduced to the reader the emotional dialect of the narrator.

Behan's self-confidence is felt again at CID headquarters: he is more concerned with the effect of his arrest on those in Ireland than with the arrest itself. Only when he is alone in his cell does he succumb to actuality. 'I looked round me. Bare concrete walls and floor. The door was a massive piece of timber and steel. The window was high up in the wall, below ground level and looking on to another wall. A bare electric bulb, over the door, shone through wire grating.' (15) The short sentences echo the loss of the prisoner's personality in the new and hostile environment. The disjunctive rhythms, like the fluid energy of the earlier passage, hint at his psychological state: they normally accompany those emotions which he feels to be a hindrance to survival— loneliness, sadness and the threat of despair.

In Walton Jail, he prefers not to use his own dialect aloud because it tends to identify his crime against England. When excited he is unable to prevent himself from shouting in an obvious Dublin accent—as, for example, with Constable Houlihan, (17)—but when he offers premeditated opposition, he does so in a rather stilted manner. The turnkey, not at all put down by Behan's standard English, abuses him roundly. Behan's reply is striking: '—you and Constable Houlihan, said I, in my own mind, and to the turnkey, "And I'll complain to the magistrate about your bad language." Now, you poxy looking ballocks, see what you make of that.' (21) The synoptic structure, placing side by side what he actually said and what he said in the safety of his own head, is used throughout the book. In the early stages it shows Behan trying to maintain his identity while avoiding the mistreatment which would follow any overt demonstration of it; later on, it enables him to qualify his amicable flattery. (e.g. 175) The clearest sign of his contentment at any time is the ease with which he uses his own accent. He had to be on guard in Walton: so eager was he to grasp the friendship proffered by a young Londoner that he became proficient in Cockney 'in two days and a bit'. (24) He longed to hear a friendly Irish accent and assumed that the Catholic chaplain would have one. But no: 'It was the accent of O'Sullivan, the detective-inspector from Cork—the Irish peasant's son trying to imitate the Lancashire lad's son whose dad 'as made a bit o' brass.' (72) In very proper English, Behan begins to answer the chaplain's criticism of the IRA, but when he is ordered to shut up, he loses all restraint. His anger is implicit in his uninhibited Dublin idioms: 'Me blood was up and me country in me knuckles . . . I might as well throw the hammer after the hatchet . . . lurry him he's no relation . . .' (75) For this assertion he is beaten up.

Before the Governor he is more circumspect. He is asked if he has heard the charges brought against him.

'I did, sir,' said I, with my hands at the seams of my trousers and looking manly, admitting my fault to this tired old consul, weary from his labours among the lesser breeds, administering the King's justice equal and fairly to wild Irish and turbulent Pathan, teaching fair play to the wily Arab and a sense of sportsmanship to the smooth Confucian. In my ballocks, said I in my own mind, you George-Arliss-headed fughpig, dull scruffy old creeping Jesus, gone past the Bengal Lancer act now back to where you started, like a got-up gentleman with his Curragh cap. Bejasus, any decent horse would drop dead if he managed to get up on his back. 'I did, sir.' (90)

The orchestration of the rhetoric is superb: the devout sympathy with the Prefect of the Empire and the subsequent demolition of the image, all done with the straight face of the opening and closing remarks. The stately balanced prose captures the languid arrogance of those whose burden it was to civilise, among others, the unruly Irish. The tone suggests that Behan has come to see the light, but this is not the case. At least one wild Irishman is holding out, delighting not in the clichés of imperialism but in the abusive argot of Dublin. Apart from the reference to George Arliss, all the components of Behan's diatribe are still current in Dublin; the author's skill lies in his ability to adapt them and combine them for his own purpose. Such passages of rhetorical abuse rise above the tenor of the early part of the novel: their distinctive images, rhythms and syntax show that despite the oppression of the penal system the prisoner maintains his native spirit. Yet he must take care: the most innocuous Hibernicism earns a rebuke from the prison doctor, while a misdirected attempt at an English colloquialism is greeted by a warder with a spit. (49, 52)

Slowly but surely, Behan is being pushed to the wall, being made to see that he must speak the language of the prison or else. Victimised by the staff, he keeps his thoughts to himself, but when the other prisoners begin to pick on the 'Killarney bastard', he realises that compromise has reached the point of diminishing returns. His reassertion of himself by means of a physical assault on another prisoner is the most sustained piece of modulated narrative in the book. It begins in despondency caused by an inability to understand the cruelty of his fellow-prisoners. It focuses on one of them, James. 'He had white-coloured hair and a sharp little nose, and though he was about twenty and maybe a little bigger than myself, I was not afraid of him. I could not say that I was not afraid of Dale because I was. He was a big well-set-up man and James only trailed after him, like a bully's labourer.' The simile from home works like an injection. 'But, by Jesus for that again, if I was afraid of the engine-driver I was not afraid of the oil-rag.' His spirits rise as he heaps abuse on James but fall as he estimates his chances of success. Then, in a memorable passage, he reminds himself that he comes from a part of Dublin which is as tough as any in the world. He brings the bag to James. 'He flung the bag in my face, and Dale laughed, and so did the fellows turning round in their seats, pleasurably, as when the curtain rises on a play.' The literary elegance of the comparison captures the mood of studied calculation and is complemented by what follows. 'I took the bag and laid it on the table and looked sorrowfully at James, miserably like Oliver Twist, to meekly and hopelessly inquire : "Please, oh, please I did nothing to you. Why are you so cruel to me?" ' This 'Irish bastard' is something more than 'gabby'; the next paragraph erupts violently.

> I led with my right hand and came up with my left, but my open palm with the metal thimble, right up into James' face. He went down and tried to hold his face down and I caught him by the hair with my right hand and held back his face while I rammed him in the face with my palm, the metal one I mean, and his blood was pouring over my hand, and the screw came rushing down . . .

Behan knows he will be punished but is clearly happy :

> And, dear dilapidated Jasus, was I going well at it till the screw caught me and pulled me off James and he went blinded and moaning and holding his hand to his face and the pouring blood. (86f.)

From now on, people will have to reckon with Behan.

His difficulties at Walton are by no means at an end but he has survived the crisis. From now onwards the tension between thought and expression will decrease. Gradually he comes to describe his situation not in the stark style already noticed but in his own ebullient vernacular. This is strikingly illustrated in his enjoyment of *Under the Greenwood Tree*: even Hardy's prose is colonised.

> Bejasus, and no one could say that Dick Dewy wasn't getting every chance of a running leap at Fancy Day. He brings over her furniture up to the new house where she's to set up as the village school-teacher; and there he was sitting on his hunkers

> trying to get the fire going till she's made the first cup of tea in the house; but by the way they were 'Yes, Mr Dewying' and 'Do you think so, Miss Daying?' they'd be there till the Lord would call them before he'd get down to introducing Fagan. And a bed and all in the house. (89)

Eventually there is no need for Behan to conceal the linguistic features which are the hallmarks of his style: his fellow-prisoners enjoy them as much as he enjoys their English slang. (e.g. 189)

It would be wrong to assume that the language of *Borstal Boy* is the everyday language of Dubliners; rather, it is a carefully chosen essence of the Dublin working-class dialect. It involves a repertoire of Dublin-accented formulae—oaths, obscenities, proverbs, stock-expressions—but it also embraces features which, though a part of the Dublin dialect, are not exclusively so. The plastic syntax and the tendency to prefer the concrete to the abstract are found in the English spoken throughout Ireland. Behan is an arranger of existing language rather than an inventor. Few of his expressions are entirely new; all are to established patterns. His rhythms are accepted by a Dubliner as accurate—the implication being that they too are traditional—but what pleases the Dubliner as much as the general reader is the manner in which they are orchestrated to accompany the narrative. Behan's great gift was his comic imagination which extended the resources of the language he inherited. The episode of the Chief Officer's disaster shows this.

It happened in Christmas week. Excommunicated, Behan remained in his cell while the other Catholics went to Confession. The monotonous rhythms catch the penal boredom:

> It was too dark to read and, anyway, I wanted to save all the reading I could for these four days, and there was a bit of white light in the sky and the snow coming, and I decided the screws might be a bit easy on us even if they caught us, it being the day before Christmas Eve, so I pulled over my table and got up [to look out the window].

The six words of the next paragraph—'And as well that I did'— introduce one of those transformations which Behan manages so well; the quickening of the pulse is felt in the introduction of the present tense, compound images and emphatic syntax.

Our Chief Officer, the stocky cruel-faced turkey-toed bastard, walks out with his glare and his strut, looking round and down at the snow, and up at the windows, five tiers of them in the square round the yard, in dead silence, and he knowing we were looking at him, and he glaring up at the barred windows, and some near me, though they must have known that he could not have seen them at that distance, got down in fear. But I did not, thank God that I did not, and those that got down must have been cutting their throats a minute later, for the next thing is, the Chief Officer, with his red-faced glare and his strut, walks clean off the steps and into six feet of snow.

The scene is set with consummate skill. The Chief Officer is described as 'turkey-toed' and this initially incredible attribute is realised in the dactyls and anapaests, *cru*-el-faced, *tur*-key-toed, with-his-*glare*, and-his-*strut*, which give the rhythms of a turkey's gait. It is amplified by the movements of the head, looking down and round and up. The Irish syntax helps to suggest the smouldering anger of this Walton Chaunticleer: 'and he *know*ing . . . and he *glar*ing' is much more emphatic than the standard 'knowing . . . and glaring', for the extra words merely accentuate the participles. The concessive clause 'though . . . distance' varies the length of the shot; 'the next thing is' zooms in on the Officer again. He is now seen as a compressed variation of his original self, his red-faced glare emphasised before total loss of identity in the snow. The surrealism of the paragraph is balanced against the concrete details: those who missed the fall were not simply disappointed, they cut their throats; it was no ordinary fall, but a walk *clean* off the steps and into *six feet* of snow.

He floundered and was lost in it, there was even hope he'd smother in it, and oh, Jesus, what a shout went up from all the windows. What delight, what joy, and as a bonus on it, didn't the old bastard, when he struggled up a step, shake his fist in anger and fall down again . . .

There is hardly any mention of the Officer or the snow: the Officer is reduced to 'he' or 'the old bastard' while the snow becomes an all-embracing 'it'. The second fall brings an ecstasy which is as palpable as money in a pay-packet. The religious element in Behan's delight is not entirely blasphemous: the excommunicated prisoner sees the hand of the Almighty in what has happened and is impressed.

> I sat down again at my table, and was thankful to God and His Blessed Mother for this.
>   If I had gone to confession, I'd have missed it, and I was consoled. God never closes one door but He opens another, and if He takes away with His right hand, He gives it back with His left, and more besides. (113-15)

The concrete imagery of the Irish proverbs lends conviction to this declaration.

Although this passage is one of the highlights, the narrative mode is typical of the book as a whole: what appears at first sight to be a transcription of colloquial delivery begins, under analysis, to show signs of careful arrangement. The storyteller has made good the disadvantages of print by varying the tempo and dynamics of his telling. This is done by means of a syntax which is much more plastic than that of standard English: paragraphs which would normally be divided into sentences are allowed to rush on without pausing for breath, while sentences which would normally be integrated by a complex of clauses are let stand in unresolved catalogue. Even where the obscenities are devoid of their etymological significance, they help to establish the rhythmical ebb and flow, and the particular accent in which they occur sets a seal of authenticity on the narrative.

The same structural control is found in the plot of the novel. *Borstal Boy*, on first reading, is a sprawling yarn, a jail journal with a simple chronological arrangement. A more careful study will show that this is not the case. A great deal of rewriting went into the book as Behan's ideas of theme and treatment became clearer. As he contemplated his life to date, he concluded that his time in England had marked him indelibly. As an idealistic and extreme nationalist he had gone to England to make war for Ireland; he had been reared in admiration of those who dedicated themselves to Ireland's freedom. He knew the consequences of arrest—torture, imprisonment, perhaps death—but he had been taught to recognise such suffering as a means to glory. He brought more than his explosives kit with him: he carried in his mind the burden of Irish history as interpreted in the songs and stories of republicanism. As expected, he was treated with some brutality;

to his surprise, he found that glory became less attractive at such a price. Other surprises were in store: he found that the English, far from being a race of ogres, were not all that different from the Irish, a mixture of good and bad. The more rigid tenets of his political faith were discarded and replaced by a generous empiricism. At the time he was unable to intellectualise the implications of his discoveries—very shortly after his release, he returned to political violence—but, later on, when he considered his drift away from political action, he felt that it was in England he had begun to face up to the falsehoods he had inherited. This was the story he would write in *Borstal Boy*, a portrait of the artist as a young prisoner.

How much of his own inner drama did Behan recognise in the exchange between Dedalus, the aspiring writer, and Davin, the enthusiastic nationalist, in Joyce's *Portrait*? Davin has asked Dedalus to be Irish first and an artist afterwards; Dedalus replies: 'When the soul of a man is born in this country there are nets flung at it to hold it back from flight. You talk to me of nationality, language, religion. I shall try to fly by those nets.'[26] In order to liberate his own soul or identity, Stephen Dedalus felt he had to disencumber himself of all his inherited prejudices and become an artist; paradoxically, only by stripping himself of his apparent Irishness could he become an Irish artist. Like Stephen, Behan's young prisoner undergoes a series of identity crises in which he is forced to question his assumptions concerning nationality and religion. In keeping with his progress through academic institutions, Stephen's development is formally pointed in symbol and intellectual terms. The growth of the prisoner's mind is less explicitly detailed. For the most part he is unaware of what is happening to him but Behan allows the reader to follow a series of unmaskings: the prisoner seeks security in poses but his experiences teach him the futility of such poses and the necessity of releasing his own basic instincts. The young lad who was arrested in Liverpool had very definite views of himself and his role but these had changed considerably on his arrival home in Dublin.

On being picked up by the detectives, Behan immediately saw the similarity between his own arrest and that of Tom Clarke. He anticipated that the sequence of events would be the same as that described by Clarke and others, with Behan in the starring role as a 'felon of our land'. Slightly disconcerted by the lack of viciousness on the part of the detectives, he comforted himself by imagining the effect which the news of his capture would have on his friends at home: 'The left-wing element in the movement would be delighted, and the others, the crawthumpers, could not say anything against me, because I was a good Volunteer, captured carrying the struggle to England's doorstep.' (13) He ends his statement with the scaffold-cry of the Manchester Martyrs in the ballad which commemorated their glorious deaths; the ballad also supplies the defiance he shows his captors.

> Girt around by cruel foes
> Still their courage proudly rose
> As they thought of them that loved them far and near,
> Of the millions true and brave
> O'er the stormy ocean's wave,
> And our friends in Holy Ireland, ever dear.

The emendation of 'their' to 'our' in the last line is telling: Behan relishes the traditional admiration which is his due. 'And all the people at home would say, reading the papers, "Ah, sure, God help poor Brendan, wasn't I only talking to him a week ago?" "By Jasus, he was a great lad all the same, and he only sixteen." ' The seriousness of his situation in Lime Street is all but forgotten in this ecstasy.

As long as he can assume this role, he is capable of taking whatever abuse is offered him. He finds it easy when 'girt around by cruel foes', but less so in the cold loneliness of his cell. He tries to relieve his physical deprivation by masturbating: 'I . . . wondered if anyone else had done it in the same condition. I didn't like to mention them by name, even in my mind. Some of them had left the cell for the rope or the firing squad.' (16) Even during the first few hours of his apotheosis, he is haunted by the very spirits who had supported him at his interrogation; they remind him that the traditional hero-prisoner should be able to resist the temptations of the flesh.

While growing up, Behan had taken for granted that, since the IRA was fighting *for* Ireland *against* England, the Volunteer could count on the support of all Irishmen and the opposition of all Englishmen. His political education and his reading of republican memoirs would have instilled into him an insistence on his status as a political prisoner; traditionally, the Volunteer listed among the hardships of confinement the contact with common criminals, the scum of England's gutter. Such neatness is not reflected in Walton Jail, at least not for Behan. One member of the prison staff is undeniably Irish, but despite his origins (or perhaps because of them), he goes out of his way to treat Behan with special harshness. On the other hand, there is Charlie, one of the common criminals, who is sympathetic and generous. Behan and Charlie become 'chinas' (mates), even though, as IRA Volunteer and Royal Navy seaman, they are technically at war with one another.

Nor is the prisoner's latent confusion limited to the question of nationality unless, in the Irish context, religion be considered an aspect of nationality. Despite consistent condemnation and mass excommunication, the average Volunteer remained staunchly Catholic, and Behan was no exception. In the gloom of his cell, he looks forward to attending mass, assuming that the priest will be Irish. Communion with the universal Church was not disappointing; it was 'like being let to the warmth of a big turf fire this cold Sunday morning'. (63) Benediction gives him the opportunity to raise his fine singing voice in clouds of incense and nostalgia and he returns to his cell a much happier boy. The sense of communion is not confined to the chapel: Charlie has solemnly declared that, even though some of the warders and prisoners 'have it in' for Behan as a member of the IRA, he is still his 'china'. The new sense of buoyancy is punctured by the priest.

The Catholic chaplain offers him an ultimatum: choose between the Church and the IRA. Behan is shattered and replies with a catalogue of the hierarchy's despotic tendencies. For the insult to the Catholic priest he is beaten up by Protestant warders. Prison regulations require that prisoners attend the services of the religion listed on their records; thus the chaplain is powerless to excommunicate Behan effectively, but he is capable of enforcing a private anathema. Religious observances were popular among prisoners as a means of breaking the monotony of their lives; especially welcome was the Friday night instruction class for R.C.s, conducted around an open fire. Ensconced in such luxury, Behan finds it hard to remain bitter and argues with himself that perhaps the priest was merely doing his duty as he saw best. When interrupted by a warder and told that, on the priest's orders, he must return to his cell, the effect is traumatic. Beatings, abuse and solitary confinement he could take, but this rejection brings him

close to tears. He bids farewell to the kind religion of his childhood and turns on the chaplain with a bitterness that is unique in
the book. 'Wasn't I the soft eedgit all the same, to expect anything more off that fat bastard of a druid? Weren't the priests
famous for backing up the warders even the time of the Fenians?
When Dr Gallagher was driven mad in Chatham Prison. (104)
In the allusion to Tom Clarke's account of Gallagher one notices
Behan retreating into the role of a 'felon of our land', a role which
had previously come under severe pressure.

After his outburst with the chaplain, Behan had been placed
in solitary confinement on bread and water. He is unwilling to
invite further abuse by showing open defiance but, typically, he
looks for heroic example in a ballad which he sings to himself.

> Some in a convict's dreary cell
> Have found a living tomb,
> And some unseen untended fell
> Within the dungeon's gloom,
> But what care we, although it be
> Trod by a ruffian band,
> God bless the clay where rest today
> The Felons of our Land.

His spiritual elevation is again subject to the weakness of the
flesh: he smells the food of which he is deprived. The novelist
succeeds in catching his hero's mental torture by following the
idealism of the ballad with a more worldly rhapsody.

> Wasn't it a great pity that the fellow that was doing the
> suffering couldn't be where the singing was to get the benefit
> of it. Mother of Christ, wasn't there a thousand places between
> Belfast and Bantry Bay where a fellow would be stuffed with
> grub, not to mind dowsed in porter, if he could only be there
> and here at the same time? But I supposed that would be like
> trying to get a drink at your own funeral. Make way there, you
> with the face, and let in the man that's doing jail for Ireland,
> and suffering hunger and abuse, let him up to the bar there.
> Oh, come up at once, the publican would say, what kind of
> men are you at all? Have you no decency of spirit about you,
> that wouldn't make way for one of the Felons of our Land?
> Come on, son, till herself gives you this plate of bacon and

cabbage, and the blessings of Jasus on you, and on everyone like you. It's my own dinner I'm giving you, for you were not expected and you among that parcel of white-livered, thin-lipped, paper-waving, key-rattling hangmen. And, come on; after your dinner there's a pint to wash it down, aye, and a glass of malt if you fancy it. Give us up a song there. Yous have enough of songs out of yous about the boys that faced the Saxon foe, but, bejasus, when there's one of them here among you, the real Ally Daly, the real goat's genollickers, yous are as silent as the tomb. Sing up, yous yous whores gets. (93f.)

Drunk on this triumph of mind over matter, the prisoner's imagination rises and swells to the tune of 'Out and Make Way for the Bold Fenian Men'. Bread and water brings him back to earth and the prisoner's physical desires are mocked by the ghost of Terence MacSwiney who starved for seventy-eight days. Volunteer Behan has come to accept his own shortcomings. What would he do if a warder offered him a round steak to sing the National Anthem of the enemy? 'Jesus, Mary, and Joseph, he'd be a lucky man that I didn't take the hand and all off him. And sing a High Mass, never mind a couple of lines of "God Save the King", for it, aye or for the half of it.' (96) Two months in Walton Jail had led him to modify some of his earlier ideas. He had not changed his mind on British imperialism but he was, for the moment, ready to settle for a tactical retreat from an exposed position. This is highlighted with hilarious clarity in his encounter with Callan.

No longer a believer in the brotherhood of all Irishmen, Behan finds Callan, who came from Monaghan, a humourless fanatic. Yet Callan, albeit arrested for theft, is a genuine IRA man and this cannot be ignored. Callan comes to prominence at a time of great danger for Behan: the execution of Barnes and McCormack is approaching and anti-Irish feeling is running high. Callan is eager to demonstrate solidarity with the doomed men, but Behan considers this futile, leading to nothing more than increased hostility and violence. Ashamed of his physical fear, he tries to lose himself in the comfortable small talk of Mrs Gaskell's *Cranford*, but his escape is shattered by the voice of Callan. He calls on Behan to declare his belief in the Republic. Frightened, Behan curses Callan, the Republic and the stolen overcoat which brought himself and Callan together. He will grant Callan's courage but wishes to excuse himself from heroism; to Callan's repeated cries for support, Behan replies with a 'discreet shout' and jumps back into bed. Questioned by warders, he meekly answers that he is reading. Then he listens as Callan is beaten. On this occasion there are no ghosts to mock him for Behan has rejected the fanaticism represented by Callan. This is not to say that he has renounced the IRA : there is no mistaking the anguish he feels at the executions in Birmingham.

> A church bell rang out a little later. They are beginning to die now, said I to myself.
> As it chimed the hour, I bent my forehead to my handcuffed right hand and made the Sign of the Cross by moving my head and chest along my outstretched fingers. It was the best that I could do. (143)

Lurking in the last sentence is the uncomfortable knowledge that his behaviour, no matter how defensible, had fallen short of that prescribed for a 'felon of our land'.

Behan's view of himself in terms of national and religious ideals has had to concede a great deal in Walton Jail; yet he realises that, no matter how much he may be forced to give in this respect, it would be disastrous to give anything in the purely physical arena. When victimised by another prisoner, he knows that he must assert himself or go under. But what self? As his masks have been stripped off one by one, he falls back on his ultimate identity.

> I was no country Paddy from the middle of the Bog of Allen to be frightened to death by a lot of Liverpool seldom-fed bastards, nor was I one of your wrap-the-green-flag-round-me junior Civil Servants that came into the IRA from the Gaelic League, and well ready to die for their country any day of the week, purity in their hearts, truth on their lips, for the glory of God and the honour of Ireland. No, be Jesus, I was from Russell Street, North Circular Road, Dublin, from the North-side, where, be Jesus, the likes of Dale wouldn't make a dinner for them, where the whole of this pack of Limeys would be scruff-hounds, would be et, bet, and threw up again—et without salt. I'll James you, you bastard. (86)

Thus roused, he attacks his taunter with a metal thimble and, luckily for himself, is restrained by warders before the victim's gang get at him. He accepts his punishment philosophically, knowing that his new reputation as tough guy is an insurance policy against utter loss of face and identity. His method was savage but one dictated by an environment in which the brutality of the warders is taken for granted and in which a prisoner is slashed with a razor on suspicion of stealing cigarette-butts.

There is a positive side to his development which now begins to emerge. He has a Crusoe-like capacity for enjoyment: prison food is often described with a relish normally reserved for higher cuisine, reading a book is an imaginative feast, while a mishap to a member of the staff provokes an orgy of pleasure. Essentially outgoing, sympathetic and humorous, his greatest delight is in friendship. Having broken through the clouds of nationalism, he senses the fellow-feeling between himself and the English boys, especially those from urban backgrounds. This is underlined at the end of the first section when he meets a sad lad named Hartigan. He assumes that because he is Liverpool-Irish, the son of an Irish Catholic, he and Behan will be 'chinas'. But Behan has learned the lesson which Hartigan has yet to learn, and he remains with the more congenial Charlie and Ginger.

The most striking element in the second section is the undisguised boyish glee with which Behan and his friends greet the change from the violence of Walton to the more liberal regime at Feltham Boys' Prison. The journey is described in language reminiscent of a boarding-school vacation; there is plenty of food at Feltham and, luxury of extravagant luxuries, Behan is given his first pair of pyjamas. He finds little difficulty in mixing with the other boys: he warms to the wit of the Londoners' rhyming slang just as they enjoy his verbal dexterity and colourful *dublinese*. His musical ability, which once tended to place him in heroic isolation, now becomes a social gift. His friends are not particularly interested in the nature of his offence—some cannot get the initials of the IRA in the correct order.

A certain amount of conflict remains. Another IRA prisoner urges Behan to adopt a superior attitude to the common criminals. Behan does not accept this advice from one who, though sound as a Volunteer, is deficient in the spirit and sense of humour which enables people to live with each other. There is no explicit comment, but Behan is clearly puzzled to discover that he has more in common with a Cockney thief than he has with a member of the IRA. He refused to join in Callan's demonstration largely because he was unwilling to invite a beating; yet he will risk physical assault to support his 'china', Charlie. With the Londoners he can swap childhood memories of hawking-cries, football matches and horse-racing lore; with them he shares a grudge against the rich. (Some prisoners suggest that Behan would do better to place explosives in the houses of the aristocracy.) He has found his place among his fellows and when one tries to stir up feeling against him because of his IRA affiliations, Behan easily dismisses him as an informer, the lowest form of prison life.

This new sense of integration flowers into one of the great set-pieces of comic literature, Holy Week at Feltham. Behan would have us believe that his excommunication enabled him to relish the ritual with atheistic objectivity, but this is not convincing. He is still sufficiently religious to have qualms about loose behaviour in church and, when he finds himself lapsing into the liturgy, he must remind himself to be disrespectful. What raises the episode above farce and into the realm of high comedy is the strong undercurrent of genuine religious feeling.

Prisoners looked forward to religious services as a relief from the dull routine of confinement and it is not surprising that non-Catholics envied the Catholics their long Easter ceremonies. Behan, a catholic Catholic, sees no just reason why his heretical friends should be deprived, on a technicality, of this opportunity for spiritual exercise: he sets himself up as a missionary, guiding a mixed bunch of pagans, protestants, atheists and agnostics into the Church for a week's free trial with no obligation to join. They are received as prison regulations demand, strictly segregated according to the amount of tobacco each was allowed: remand prisoners (twenty a day) sat in front, those in solitary (none) at the back, the others ranged in between. The neo-Catholics show an expert understanding of the Passion: after all, like themselves, Jesus was arrested on information received, charged and convicted in very unfair circumstances. They revile the informer Judas and warmly approve of Peter's desire to inflict grievous bodily harm on him. 'Carve the bastard up.' The essence of the comedy is not any blasphemous rowdyism but the lively link between Jesus and the prisoners: they show an awareness of his

suffering more informed, intense and imaginative than that normally found in 'outside' churches. And they are the lost ones for
whom Jesus expressed special concern.

On Good Friday, the Italian priest, equally excited, asks the
prisoners to accompany him around the Stations of the Cross.
The warders are dumbfounded at the breach of regulations but
helpless against the priest's command. As the prisoners mingle in
a new communal ecstasy, those that have minister unto those that
have not. The pastoral reputation of the Catholic Church was
never so high and the amazing priest who is partly responsible
for this glimpse of paradise is very properly rewarded in the little
final paragraph which encapsulates the uplift of spirit which our
hero has enjoyed at Feltham Boys' Prison:

> On Easter Sunday the little priest skipped round the altar like a
> spring lamb and gave a triumphant sermon in gleaming white
> and gold vestments and the sun shining through the window on
> him. (201)

Ecce Agnus Dei. . . .

The novel takes its title from the third and final section which
deals with the time spent in Hollesley Bay Borstal Institution. On
the way there, Behan regales his friends with popular and Irish
patriotic songs. There is no longer any need for him to soft-pedal
his membership of the IRA. When he gives a fervently obscene
account of an IRA victory over the Black and Tans the others
admire his wit and applaud his insubordination.

These boys have been judged unfit for human society, yet Behan
does not consider himself a criminal and his friends are singularly
free from the remorse of conscience which their confinement is
intended to incite. Behan remarks that a prisoner's crime was only
alluded to as a means of description; a more amusing expression
of this most Christian charity is the tale of the boy, convicted of
forgery, who won the cross-country race in an unusual manner.

> . . . the long forger's legs of him and his beaky counterfeit
> nose brought him in before anyone else, also due to conservation
> of his energies behind the incinerators, where he slyly hid and
> rested himself while the other honest poor bastards—well, by
> comparison, poor simple robbers and rapers and murderers—
> went round the second time. (279)

Objections are overruled on the grounds that he deserved his prize—fifty cigarettes—for his cunning if not for his athletic prowess. These boys, although condemned for serious crimes such as murder, rape and forgery, demand some sympathy. They react differently to different environments. In Walton Jail it was necessary to be vicious in order to survive; in the more enlightened atmosphere of Hollesley Bay, the behaviour is proportionately more civilised, for most of these boys found for the first time in the Governor of Hollesley Bay an authority they could respect. Compared to Walton Jail, Hollesley Bay was a boarding-school: there are abuses and punishments but, although it is an open Borstal, only one boy tries to escape.

The role of the escaper is rather similar to that of Hartigan in the opening section: in analysing him, Behan tells us a good deal about his own condition. The boy who escapes is an upper class *toff* who suffers more than most because he is isolated in a mainly working-class milieu.

> He was dead lonely; more lonely than I and with more reason. The other fellows might give me a rub about Ireland or about the bombing campaign, and that was seldom enough, and I was never short of an answer, historically informed and obscene, for them. But I was nearer to them than they would ever let Ken be. I had the same rearing as most of them, Dublin, Liverpool, Manchester, Glasgow, London. Our mothers had all done the pawn pledging on Monday, releasing on Saturday. We all knew the chip shop and the picture house and the fourpenny rush of a Saturday afternoon, and the summer swimming in the canal and being chased along the railway by the cops. (241f.)

Remembering his own isolation, Behan sympathises with the lonely aristocrat, even when it displeases his 'chinas'.

The question of class becomes prominent in the third section. On his arrest, Behan had made left-wing noises but, in retrospect, they seem to have been a part of his pose rather than firm convictions. In Borstal he has a series of political discussions with a socialist from Blackpool. He supports the Irish people but condemns the IRA for failing to see that their fight was not with England but with the class-structure of capitalism. He urges Behan to see himself as a member of the working class and therefore superior to the other prisoners who would steal rather than work and who are, eventually, 'a dirty degenerate lot of scum' (303). Behan is unable to counter these arguments in intellectual terms— which is surprising when one considers his consistent pride in his intelligence and loquacity—but his emotions do not allow him to disclaim his 'chinas'. This socialist strangled his own girlfriend, hardly a character reference for the apostle of the brotherhood of workers, but Behan's rejection is based not on his criminal record but on his lack of humour. The other prisoners do not like the conceited strangler.

> And small blame to them, with your scrawny face and your red Anti-Christ's stubble on it, and the miserable undertaker's labourer's chat out of you; wouldn't it be the eighth wonder of the world if anyone would go within the bawl of an ass you, except for the judy that got within strangling distance, bejasus? . . . I had no mother to break her heart, and I had no china to take my part, but I had one friend and a girl was she, that I croaked with her own silk stocking. (355)

Nevertheless, this unfortunate has helped Behan to clarify his own ideas: when accused by a Scot of liking the English despite their behaviour in Ireland, he replies that it is the imperialist system which persecutes Ireland and that some of its most obnoxious lackeys are Irish and Scots.

In the relative security of Hollesley Bay, a more thoughtful side of the prisoner becomes apparent. His essay on Dublin wins a prize and his sensitivity produces *en passant* some fine pieces of natural description.

> The autumn got weaker and beaten, and the leaves all fell, and a bloody awful east wind that was up before us and we on our way to work in the morning, sweeping down off the top of the North Sea, which in the distance looked like a bitter band of deadly blue steel out along the length of the horizon, around the freezing marshes, the dirty grey shore, the gun-metal sea, and over us the sky, lead-coloured for a few hours, till the dark fell and the wind rose, and we went down the road from work at five o'clock in the perishing evening. (359)

This cold pastoral reflects an element in the prisoner's character which one takes more and more for granted as the book progresses. His farewell to Borstal is not a broadside of merry obscenity: the tone is confused but the nostalgia is evident.

> I'd have thought our Matron would have been there, and was disappointed that she was not, but, all of a hurry, just as we started the car, she came rushing to the doorway and waved a half-knitted sock, and I waved frantically back, and that was the last I saw of Borstal. Though she wasn't given a chance of saying good-bye to me not a bad picture was our Matron, to carry away with me. (377)

The news of his release comes as a shock both to Behan and to the reader. The boy at boarding-school will count the last weeks, days, hours and minutes, but Behan does not. As a prisoner of war, his first duty was to escape. His claim that the odds against success were enormous is credible but not altogether convincing. Gradually one concludes that he enjoyed his time in Hollesley Bay. He does not dispute the Governor's boast that Borstal had made a man of him. It had certainly taught him a great deal about himself and about life in general: it had sharpened his perception, taught him to use his comic gifts as a means of survival, granted him leisure to read widely and given him his first literary award. The matron with the half-knitted sock was the crest of his *alma mater*.

Sailing into Dublin Bay, he counts the hills and spires, remarking that they are there as if he had never left them. This is a complex observation, part of the complexity being the prisoner's subconscious surprise that anything could have stayed the same when he had changed so much. He is uncertain what other changes await him: the immigration official welcomes him quietly in Irish, the detective on the gangway is silent.

6

An Giall and *The Hostage*

As the successful author of *The Quare Fellow*, Behan accepted commissions to write two plays, *The Big House* for BBC radio and *An Giall* for Gael Linn.

The Big House, broadcast in 1957, has often been criticised as sub-standard, and justly so if *The Quare Fellow* is the standard, but such a comparison is unfair.[1] *The Big House* is a romp and excellent as such. To see it as 'an allegory of sorts' is to risk missing the fun.[2] The story is reminiscent of O'Casey's *Purple Dust*, but the treatment is pure Behan. An Anglo-Irish couple are forced to leave their mansion during the Irish Civil War; the place is plundered by a Dubliner and a Cockney who celebrate afterwards in a Dublin pub. More important than the plot is the farcical spirit of the piece, the songs, the jokes and the conversations of two *oul' wans*, Granny Grunt and Granny Growl. A good deal of the humour would be lost on a non-Irish audience and this, too, is part of the fun. For example, the house is named Tonesollock, the Irish for Dirtybum. In the previous year Behan had shaken the British establishment by appearing drunk on BBC television; now, in the same iconoclastic vein, he was pushing broadmindedness to its limits. The play opens and closes with the house intoning its concern for 'my bullocks, oh, my bullocks'.[3] This should be enough to warn off those who would trespass in search of deep meanings: the author has enjoyed himself but knows that it is all bull or all balls.

It is the sort of thing which he could improvise in a bar, trusting to his wild imagination, his exuberant sense of humour and his ability to resurrect the spirit of the Northside, an extension of sketches he wrote in his time as a journalist.

Granny Growl: Ah me tired husband, he was in the Boer War,

E

and he was standing there in the middle of South Africa, in a big long line, thousands upon thousands of them, stiff as pokers, not a man to move even when a comrade fell, stretched on the parade ground, prostituted from the heat, and up rides Lord Roberts.

Granny Grunt: A lovely man. I seen him in the Park and a pair of moustaches on his face a yard long. Waxed and stiff, they went through me boozem.

Granny Growl: He rides along half the length of the line till he comes to my Paddins, and lets a roar out of him that would move your bowels: 'Fusilier Kinsella!' he roars.

Granny Grunt: God bless us!

Granny Growl: 'Fusilier Kinsella', he shouts. Paddins steps forward, smacks the butt of his rifle, and Lord Roberts looks down at him off his big white horse, and his moustache trembling with glory. 'Fusilier Kinsella', he roars, 'wipe your bayonet . . . you've killed enough!'⁴

The entire performance is professional in the best sense. At the time Behan was concentrating on his novel but the BBC offered kudos and easy money. Shrewdly, Behan drew on the material he had written for the *Irish Press* and on the technical experience he gained in Radio Éireann and turned out a first class job which has not yet lost its zest or lustre.

In 1956, Gael Linn, the Irish language organisation which produced *Comhar*, opened a small theatre in Dublin. In March 1957, Behan undertook to write a play for them, retaining the full translation rights himself;⁵ *An Giall* opened to favourable reviews in June 1958. His decision to write for Gael Linn must have surprised his literary mentors abroad. *The Quare Fellow*, rejected by the major theatres in Dublin, had made Behan an author of international standing: it was due to be staged in New York, Paris and Berlin. *Borstal Boy*, on which he was working during 1957, promised to be an enormous success: the American rights were being negotiated. Fame and fortune were at hand. In 1958 he travelled to Ibiza to begin a new novel, to Paris to discuss the French production of *The Quare Fellow*, and to Sweden where he put the finishing touches to *Borstal Boy*. If wealth and acclaim were his only objectives, Gael Linn had little to offer—a tiny theatre and the obscurity of a relatively unknown language. But there was, as has been shown, another side to Behan, quieter and less materialistic. He felt indebted to Gael Linn for support during his leaner days and he was attracted to their theatre. When he had written *Casadh Súgáin Eile* he had imagined himself as the dramatist of a new Gaelic revival; his poetry witnesses a dream of an Ireland which was not only physically but spiritually independent. No amount of foreign applause could satisfy this facet of his personality: he could no more forget his earlier hopes than he could cut himself off completely from the IRA. He had always wanted, among other things, to serve Ireland and now, as something of a world figure, he was in a strong position to do so.

Attached to *An Giall* are stories of haste and carelessness, partly based on fact, partly spread by Behan himself: the original producer complained that the play came in dribs and drabs, 'scrawled on the backs of cornflake bags', while Behan said that he wrote the play in twelve days.[6] Despite all this, *An Giall* is a well-made piece and was immediately recognised as such by the critics: '*An Giall* is a very cleverly written play. Indeed, in the first act the writing was possibly too clever and the dialogue was overloaded with witty lines that were of little use to the play as a whole. However, this was a small fault and did not detract from the overall picture of excellence.'[7] Audiences were equally impressed.

The plot is simple. A young IRA Volunteer has been sentenced to death in Belfast for the shooting of two policemen. The IRA kidnap a young English soldier from Armagh barracks and hold him as a hostage in Dublin, threatening to kill him if the Volunteer is executed. There is some suggestion in the play that the IRA is bluffing, but the soldier dies, smothered in a closet into which he was bundled during a police raid. (Behan wrote that the play was based on an incident in Northern Ireland when the IRA found themselves with an unwanted hostage whom they later released; Seamus de Burca, more convincingly, relates the plot to an episode during the Suez Canal invasion, when a British officer was captured and later found dead, smothered in a press.[8]) The similarity in theme between this play and *The Quare Fellow* is obvious. This time the execution is political. We meet the *quare fellow* and find that, behind all the political argument, he is no *quarer* than ourselves—just a young, shy, brave boy who does not want to die. Again, it is the impersonal system which is repulsive. The soldier is to suffer not for anything which he has done himself, but because he is an English soldier. He was legally bound to do his National Service; actually, he volunteered beforehand because volunteers had an easier time and more money. The dramatist is at pains to stress the personal reality of the lad as opposed to his political image. As in *The Quare Fellow*, there is one important character who does not appear physically on the stage, the doomed Volunteer. The radio gives his name but nothing else, apart from his crime and appointed punishment. This under-writing is dramatically successful: during the play the audience begins to suspect that the lad in Belfast is almost certainly somebody like the soldier, bewildered and frightened by his circumstances, yet accepting death with desperate dignity. To some, Michael Kevin O'Neill and Leslie Williams are real human beings; to others, they are pawns in an all-important struggle. O'Neill's fate is discussed by those who are holding Leslie:

> *Patrick*: It could be worse.
> *Kate*: How could it be worse?
> *Patrick*: If I was in his place.
> *Monsewer*: What's that? I beg your pardon?
> *Patrick*: I'm saying that this young man will be in the company of Pearse and the other heroes a few minutes after eight tomorrow morning.
> *Monsewer*: He will, he will indeed, with the help of God. In the company of the heroes. It brings joy to my heart.
> *He blows on the pipes and sounds a note. Then he begins to sing.* (14)[9]

The song is one which Behan had written in 1946 in honour of Sean McCaughey, an IRA officer who had died on hunger-strike.[10] That Behan should now give it to the ridiculous Monsewer shows how much he had changed in twelve years. *An Giall* dramatises the tension between those who see political martyrdom as something glorious and those who see human life as too exorbitant a price for any political objective.

An Giall is as much concerned with time and age as it is with patriotism, love or death. The list of characters provides only names (or titles) and ages—with one exception: Patrick is one-legged. Monsewer, aged 70, is the most flamboyant and the only one who could have taken part in the 1916 Rising. He wears a kilt and plays bagpipes in the mistaken belief that they are Irish. In fact, they are more properly Scottish but, as with his name, Monsewer is more interested in emphasising his unEnglishness. The son of an English bishop, he enjoyed the privileges of the English aristocracy—public school, Oxford, wealth and pleasure —until, discovering that he was of Irish descent, he turned to Irish dancing on Clapham Common and subsequently fought against the English in 1916. An implacable republican, he accepted neither the Treaty nor the order to lay down arms but insisted on continuing the war of independence. He owns the house in which the action takes place. In order to make ends meet, his loyal lieutenant, Patrick, has begun to take in prostitutes and petty criminals as lodgers. Monsewer believes that they are republicans and that their frequent prison sentences are for political offences. Monsewer is mad, living in a world of his own where time has stood still for almost half a century, blind to the reality around him.

Kate cannot understand why Patrick remains loyal to Monsewer.

Kate: Aren't you always telling me he's mad?
Patrick: He wasn't always mad. (*Thinking.*) He wasn't mad when I saw him first, or anything like it, God bless him. (5)

He does not deny that Monsewer is mad, but he is unable to forget what a fine man he was before the Treaty of 1921 upset his mental balance. Like Monsewer, Patrick is trapped by the glorious past but not to the same extent. He sees what is happening around him. He is disenchanted with the IRA of today but, unable to find anything admirable in his own situation, holds on to the splendour of better days gone by. His schizophrenia is cruelly obvious in his physical handicap: he must walk with a stick, having lost a leg in the Civil War which followed the Treaty. He recalls the incident:

Patrick: Good men from both sides were lost. Genuinely brave fighters, not like the shower of jackeens on the go today. (*Almost to himself, remembering the heroic past.*) For three days non-stop the battle raged with terrible ferocity. Ourselves and the West-Limerick Brigade. Lewis machine-guns,

Thomson sub-machine-guns, mortars, grenades, revolvers and rifles, the town blazing and the dead on the road.

Kate: You told me before that only one man was killed. The Westmeath County Surveyor who wasn't bothering anybody but was measuring the roads. Didn't you tell me that both sides claimed him after the war and that they erected two memorial crosses to him: one on each side of the road.

Patrick: You don't care what I said.

Kate: That's your version, especially when you're drunk. But like most of the men in this country, that's the only time you tell the truth. (4)

This dreamed-up account of the battle is Patrick's antidote against the unacceptable reality of his life, depending on robbers, whores and criminals for subsistence, being used by an organisation which has no time for the socialism which once attracted him.

Patrick's innate generosity shines through his political prejudices and general confusion. He will fulminate against prostitutes but he himself is obviously in love with the whore Kate. He is unable to embrace her with youthful vigour, but puts his hand on her shoulder:

. . . I wasn't thinking of you at all. You know that. Aren't we —aren't we married—almost.

Kate: We are, Patrick, we're married—almost. (7)

He resents the prim piousness of the IRA Officer and demands the usual terms for his use of the house; yet he offers him food and drink. It is refused.

Officer: I don't drink, thank you.

Volunteer: Me neither.

Officer: Except maybe a bottle of orange and me sweating after a High Cauled Cap at a *céilí* in the Mansion House. (34)

Patrick is essentially kind, even to the English soldier, trying to set him at his ease and furthering the friendship which grows between the soldier and Teresa, the serving-girl. This kindness he shares with Kate, the traditional whore with a heart of gold.

The house in which the action takes place is known as The Hole. The dramatic implications are not only sensual: the house is gradually felt to represent the psychological darkness of those who inhabit it. It is a trap, a *cul-de-sac* off the main avenue of life. Monsewer is master, blind to everything except the imaginary light of an obsolete campaign. The IRA Officer and Volunteer are equally oblivious to all except 'the cause': they are shadowy and negative, humourless and almost impersonal in their political devotion. In the intolerance of love and kindness they are as insane as Monsewer. Patrick and Kate are not insane, but they are trapped, Patrick (aged 68) by his loyalty to Monsewer and an ideal past, Kate (aged 38) by her loyalty to Patrick and by the social circumstances which drove her to prostitution. Accidentally, two young people find themselves in this limbo, one as a political hostage, the other as a maid.

Teresa's life has been hard: having been orphaned she was brought up by nuns to be a menial. Yet she has retained her innocence and sensitivity. Hers is a positive and resilient innocence which makes her immune to the spiritual and social corrosion of The Hole. Though normally meek and deferential to her elders, she is not afraid to speak her mind.

Teresa: Monsewer is daft.
Kate: Monsewer daft? Girl, you don't know what you're saying. Monsewer was at the great colleges of England.
Teresa: It's all the same where he was. He's mad—saying that the death of a young man brought joy to his heart.
Kate: Well, didn't the boy himself, in the speech he made in court when he was sentenced to death, say that he was glad to die for Ireland? Do you think he's daft?
Teresa: He's very young. He's innocent. He doesn't know about life.
Kate: You do—a young girl of eighteen?
Teresa: I don't suppose that boy was ever out with a girl, that he knows the delight of being young—and the heartbreak. He gave all his love to Ireland and instead of breaking his heart over a girl, it's because of the country he's breaking it. (15)

Teresa is not quite as sure of herself as she pretends. She cannot refute the political arguments, but she is impervious to abstract idealism, convinced of the supreme importance of life and love.

Towards the end of the first act, Teresa prevails on Kate to join her as she dances to a tune, 'The Blackbird', being played on the radio. Unknown to them, the door is opened to reveal an English soldier. When they become aware of his presence they stop.

> *Soldier*: Don't stop. I like dancing.
> *He is cheerful, relaxed, smiling. He enters, the Officer and another man after him. They keep their right hands in their pockets.* (16)

The audience will to some extent have judged the soldier in his absence. They probably expect a professional, toughened by his chosen career and his experiences of war in Northern Ireland, his hostility to the Irish increased by his kidnapping. Consequently, his nonchalance is surprising, his friendliness disarming. His very ordinariness contrasts with the sinister discipline of his captors. He asks the IRA Officer if his tea will be brought by the young girl, Teresa.

> *Officer*: (*Looking around at the Volunteer*) I suppose so.
> *Soldier*: Great. (*Looks delightedly at the Officer but gets no reply from his countenance; looks at the Volunteer but gets no reply from him either; he gets no reaction at all, does not understand them but says nothing; he sighs.*) That's all. (17)

His relationship with Teresa is more promising and is the basis of the second act.

She sees him, not as an anonymous element in a power-struggle, but as an attractive young man. 'She assumes a very sensible air, speaking to him as a mother, which is not very satisfactory from his point of view.' When he establishes that he is in fact seven months older than her, she counters with a directness that is not entirely jocular:

> *Teresa*: (*seriously*) You're not all that old . . . indeed, we'd make a good couple.

Noticing his embarrassment, she becomes friendlier, using the informal 'what will we call you?' instead of the standard 'what is your name?' In the latter part of the second act, they dispense with shyness and pretence and find in each other the first love of their lives. Behind their conversation one sometimes hears Mon-

sewer playing the wailing lament called 'The Flowers of the
Forest'. He is planning to lament the death in Belfast, but the
audience knows that if there is one death there will be two, and
cannot fail to see that the love of Leslie and Teresa is blooming
in the shadow of death.

There is an element of dramatic irony in their political discussions: Leslie's attitude is similar to that which Teresa showed
to Kate in the first act, while Teresa now repeats the objections
formerly raised by Kate. Leslie thinks Monsewer is mad and
argues that British mistreatment of Ireland is a thing of the past,
like Julius Caesar. 'Everybody was doing something to everybody
in those days.' He is neither disingenuous nor stupid.

> *Leslie*: It's the Irish, not the English, who will hang [the lad
> in Belfast]. And after all, although I feel sorry for the poor
> fellow, you have to admit he shot two policemen. You can't
> let people get away with that sort of thing or there'd be no
> law or order. If an Englishman had done it, he'd be hanged
> too.
> *Teresa*: He was fighting on account of the English being in
> Ireland.
> *Leslie*: Aren't there Irishmen in England? (23)

They turn from political to personal considerations and discover
that they are both orphans. They move closer to one another,
stumbling over such barriers as religion, polite language and the
proverbial unreliability of soldiers' promises. Here again Leslie
belies the common image; he has never had a girlfriend and longs
for a photograph which he could show off in the barracks. Teresa
provides one with the mandatory kiss-signs. She also gives him
a medal of devotion not to military heroism but to the Blessed
Virgin. In return, he gives what he can, kisses and affection, and
the act comes to a close as they celebrate their union with a dance
—not to the traditional music of Ireland but to the more universal
and youthful rhythms of rock 'n' roll. Their private idyll is soon
interrupted: the radio which provided the music now announces
the decision of the IRA to kill Leslie if the prisoner in Belfast is
executed.

Leslie is unable to see anything glorious in the possibility of
being shot. He has no illusions.

> *Leslie*: Do you think they're sitting around in their West End

F

clubs crying for me? Do you think that the Secretary of State for War will say to his wife: 'Isabelle Cynthia dear, I can't sleep thinking about poor Williams.' Well, I've always heard that the Irish were daft but I never knew till now just how daft they were. (30)

He does not believe what Patrick tells him: that he is being held merely as a threat and that nobody intends to carry out the threat. His trained eye picks out the IRA guard on the house. Despite his lack of idealism, he is courageous and even a little patriotic: 'Maybe we don't go on with as much gab about dying, but we are as brave as anybody else' (31). Only his love for Teresa can take his mind off the danger, allowing him to make plans for a future with her. Her love for him is her strongest loyalty: she is willing (but unable) to leave the house and contact the police.

The end is sudden. Leslie is bound, gagged and bundled into a closet. The sound of shooting and of engines is followed by a police raid on the house. Having failed to find anything in the house, the police depart. When the closet is opened, Leslie is dead of suffocation. As the others in the house try to excuse themselves, Teresa embraces him:

Teresa: Leslie is dead, dead. You killed him.
Patrick: Teresa, we didn't wish to.
Teresa: He's dead.
Officer: Well now, in Belfast Prison—
Patrick: Yes, Teresa, in the Six Counties—
Teresa: It wasn't the six counties that were bothering you. You were trying to get back two things which you can't get back—your youth and your lost leg.
(*Still sitting on the floor.*) There was none of your own people to cry for you, my darling. I'll be a little mother for you, a little sister for you, and I'll love you and I'll never forget you. (*Breaking into tears.*) Never.

An Giall is not notable for its linguistic colour, and only one of the characters, Monsewer, is portrayed with the extravagance one associates with Behan. What contributes most to the success of the play is the imaginative generosity of the dramatist. No character or group of characters has a monopoly of what may be

understood as Behan's own opinions; in every character, even
Monsewer, aspects of Behan's personality are reflected. In the
Officer and Volunteer one senses that extreme idealism which
fired Behan at Glasnevin. Monsewer is an exaggeration to ab-
surdity of Behan's own inability to free himself from the imagery
of his childhood. Patrick may be seen as a projection of what
Behan might have become as a result of his political affiliations.
Like his creator, Patrick inclined to the left wing of the republican movement, rejected the prim puritanism of the right and
became disenchanted with the later IRA; nevertheless, both were
trapped by their previous involvement. Like Patrick, Behan knew
what it was like to be restricted by social circumstances, and, like
Patrick, Behan often found that his impulsive kindness took him
across political divisions. The younger people in the play give
some indication of Behan's hopes of a fresh future. Surprisingly
enough, when Behan is considered as the quintessential Dubliner
and staunch republican, this new generation is comprised of a
simple country girl and a British Army private. It would be a
mistake to assume that Teresa and Leslie are Behan's mouth-
pieces: like Monsewer and all the others, they are merely parts
of a complex vision. The plot shows how difficult it was to opt
out of the political reality. *An Giall* and the contemporary *Borstal
Boy* suggest that Behan was becoming more and more convinced
of the dangers inherent in strict ideologies, not only for the
disciple but also for those who crossed his path.

An Giall never becomes propagandist: it is a play, not a tract.
It would be wrong to describe it as *pro-* or *anti-*IRA. Nobody
takes Monsewer and the Officer to be accurate representations of
the IRA, any more than anybody believes Leslie's attitude to
Ireland to be that of the British government. The characters are,
at once, individuals of a specific time and place, and symbols of
an action which is not defined by time or place: in one sense
they are dwarfed by the political conflict between Britain and
Ireland, in another sense they show the insignificance of this
squabble in the universal history of conflict. The play is concerned with ideology rather than politics. It presents two sets of
people, those who have been scarred and those who are crushed
by ideology. Against a background of extremism and insanity,
two couples are shown struggling for life, Patrick and Kate,
Leslie and Teresa. The couples are distinguished by age. Patrick

and Kate, for social and psychological reasons, have failed to break away from The Hole. Leslie and Teresa, with their powers of sympathy and imagination, seem capable of escaping the drab fate which their births ordained for them. Instead they suffer even more than Patrick and Kate. The tragedy is aggravated by the nature of Leslie's death, accidentally killed during an ineffectual raid.

An Giall, though it lacks the verbal power and the visual impact of *The Quare Fellow*, succeeds within its scope. Behan has dramatised the poignancy of two young people caught in a conflict which they neither desire nor comprehend. It is an old theme and, though he renewed its appeal by locating it in contemporary Ireland, he added little to it. Monsewer is a memorable character; Leslie and Teresa are very satisfactory but we have known many such pairs of 'star-crossed lovers' before. Given a sympathetic production it retains its power to inspire pity and fear.

The Hostage

Towards the end of the second act of *The Hostage*, Pat, the Officer and Leslie discuss the author:

Soldier: Brendan Behan, he's too anti-British.

Officer: Too anti-Irish, you mean. Bejasus, wait till we get him back home. We'll give him what-for for making fun of the Movement.

Soldier: (*to audience*). He doesn't mind coming over here and taking your money.

Pat: He'd sell his country for a pint.

(*What happens next is not very clear. There are a number of arguments all going on at once. Free-Staters against Republican, Irish against English, homosexuals against heterosexuals, and in the confusion all the quarrels get mixed up and it looks as though everyone is fighting everyone else. In the centre of the melee, MISS GILCHRIST is standing on the table singing 'Land of Hope and Glory'. The IRA OFFICER has one chair and is waving a Free State flag and singing 'The Soldier's Song', while the RUSSIAN SAILOR has the other and sings the Soviet National Anthem. The NEGRO parades through the room carrying a large banner inscribed 'KEEP IRELAND BLACK'. The piano plays throughout. Suddenly the* VOLUNTEER *attacks the* SOLDIER *and the* RUSSIAN *joins in the fight. The* VOLUNTEER *knocks* MULLEADY's *bowler hat over his eyes and* ROPEEN *flattens the* VOLUNTEER. MULLEADY *is now wandering around blind with his hat over his eyes, and holding* ROPEEN's *aspidistra. The* VOLUNTEER, *somewhat dazed, sees the* RUSSIAN's *red flag and thinks he has been promoted to guard. He blows his railway whistle and the fight breaks up into a wild dance in which they all join on the train behind the* VOLUNTEER *and rush round the room in a circle. All this takes about a minute and a half . . .) (*76f.)[11]

What happened to *An Giall*?

Joan Littlewood, who was responsible for a splendid production of *The Quare Fellow*, was keen that Behan should translate *An Giall* so that she could stage it in London. Behan was happy to oblige. (*The Hostage* opened in October, four months after the premier of *An Giall* at the Damer.) Miss Littlewood was unable to read the original script, but presumably she had a good idea of the nature and style of *An Giall*; if so, it would seem that she had much more than a straight translation in mind. An *avant garde* producer, noted for her theatrical imagination and her social conscience, she would hardly have been content to repeat in English the traditional naturalism of *An Giall*. Her theatre was a genuine workshop, a community in which nobody was allowed to dominate. The dramatist was simply a member of the team and his script was by no means sacrosanct. The Theatre Workshop used the script as a basis, cutting what they thought weak, emending as they saw fit, and adding in material which they thought relevant. The objectives were not new—to please and instruct—but the method was. In order to gain the attention and goodwill of the audience, jokes and references to current events were included; a rapport established, 'messages' of philanthropy, tolerance, liberation and equality were promulgated. Even those who did not agree with Joan Littlewood's methods had to admit that the end-result was exciting theatrical entertainment; the box-office proved it.[12] Her *Quare Fellow* was, for all practical purposes, the play as Behan submitted it.[13] She used the resources and techniques of the Theatre Workshop to realise

Behan's script. A different relationship obtained during the rehearsals of *The Hostage.*

By the summer of 1958 The Theatre Workshop was in financial trouble and needed a 'hit'. No author seemed more capable of providing one than Behan: the applause for *The Quare Fellow* still echoed, he claimed headlines at will, his new novel was about to be published and his second play had been well received in Dublin. Behan was indebted, as he saw it, to Joan Littlewood and it only remained for him to present her with an English version of *An Giall*. This did not happen. Behan was unable to concentrate on translation: he was still trying to complete *Borstal Boy*, his desire to see the book in print competing with his desire to taste the fruits of his recent fame. Two months before *The Hostage* was due to open, very little of the play existed. 'What happens next is not very clear.' It would seem that he decided to accommodate Joan Littlewood, providing the basis of a workshop play rather than a script in the traditional sense. This was partly because he admired her methods and sympathised with her views. He later said:

> Joan Littlewood, I found, suited my requirements exactly. She has the same views on the theatre that I have, which is that the music hall is the thing to aim at for to amuse people and any time they get bored, divert them with a song or a dance. I've always thought T. S. Eliot wasn't far wrong when he said that the main problem of the dramatist today was to keep his audience amused; and that while they were laughing their heads off, you could be up to any bloody thing behind their backs; and it was what you were doing behind their bloody backs that made your play great.[14]

This was his public opinion more than a year after the success of *The Hostage*; one wonders if he was quite so sure of himself beforehand. The evidence suggests that his willingness to collaborate with the Theatre Workshop was also due to his inability to rewrite the play himself which may, in turn, have been because he doubted if *An Giall* could repeat the triumph of *The Quare Fellow*. The script was late and incomplete: gaps invited the company to influence the play as they wished. During rehearsals, it evolved into a mutated version of *An Giall*.

Joan took a play to pieces and she put it back together again
with actors' inserts, ad libs and catch phrases. Sometimes it
worked, sometimes it didn't. Often in rewriting, the original
idea was lost. I had to fight her for the survival of script . . .
Brendan didn't care. He was pissed out of his mind anyway
when half the changes were made. It was only when you saw
The Quare Fellow you realised what a good writer he was and
how much better his work could be than the changes he accepted from Littlewood. A lot of the non-sequitur scenes were
invented by Joan.[15]

Even playwrights who stood out against the Workshop's approach were never totally successful. Behan offered no resistance
and even contributed to the metamorphosis of his play.

It is impossible to say just how different *The Hostage* is or was.
Even during its first run, the play was a variable: it was altered
to suit the theatre and the night, topical references changing from
place to place and time to time. The printed edition is simply the
script at the time of publication: footnotes on pages 53 and 54
suggest that social allusions be kept up to date. To what extent
may the work be attributed to Behan? Even if it could be established that every word in the script was written or dictated by
him, there remains the question: whose idea was it to transform
the original play?

An Giall was, essentially, a naturalistic tragedy; *The Hostage*
is a musical extravaganza. Characters were added—two male
homosexuals, two whores, a Civil Servant, a social worker and a
Russian sailor—and the action studded with songs so that a pianist
was required on-stage. This is, one supposes, quite in order in a
Dublin brothel, but the behaviour of the visitors is obviously
designed to suit a London audience of the late fifties, when even
the mention of homosexuality in the theatre was considered
daring and revolutionary. This element of shock is likely to be
lost on a modern audience, as are the references to Sister Rowe,
Uffa Fox, Jayne Mansfield, Macmillan and Kruschev. Between
flauntings and floutings the original plot advances in disguise.
Pat describes the raid in a manner reminiscent of Mickser in *The
Quare Fellow*. Leslie is shot. Teresa mourns him as in *An Giall*.

*A ghostly green light glows on the body as Leslie Williams
slowly gets up and sings . . . The stage brightens, and every-*

one turns and comes down towards the audience, singing:

> The bells of hell,
> Go ting-a-ling-a-ling,
> For you but not for him,
> Oh death, where is thy sting-a-ling-a-ling!
> Or grave thy victory. (108f.)

The resurrection of Leslie asserts some kind of a victory of life over death and effects a comic resolution of the action. In the circumstances, the tragic finale of *An Giall* would have been stylistically discordant and melodramatic. (The close of *The Hostage* may also be taken as an ironic comment on theatrical naturalism.) The resolution is good for a laugh but seems facile if compared with previous dramatic resurrections—for example, in Euripides' *Alkestis* and Shakespeare's *Winter's Tale,* where more experienced playwrights took much greater pains. In these plays, the sting of death and the grave's victory had already been established with all their pains and horrors. In *The Hostage,* death had always been something of a throw-away line; consequently, Leslie's death does not make an impression sufficiently strong to serve as the basis for the final miracle.

The Workshop *Hostage* was a huge success. The English critics enjoyed themselves as much as the audience. Even those people, mostly Irish, who went to the play expecting to be embarrassed by the rumoured prostitution of Behan's talent, were more often than not disarmed and won over by the infectious hilarity. Seasoned drama critics were enthusiastic almost to the extent of impropriety: they wrote of the intoxicating freshness which *The Hostage* exuded. It was as if they had not laughed for years. 'It was a rare and invigorating experience.' The play was so entertaining that they were prepared to excuse 'a multitude of shamelessly loose touches'. One, by no means ill disposed to what he had seen, wrote: 'more than half the time it turns to undisguised cabaret. . . . It's magnificent, but it isn't drama.'[16] Such a view is always in danger of being decried as negative, conservative, reactionary or, most damning of all, academic; it is none the less interesting for that.

The twin aims of the Theatre Workshop were to divert and instruct. *The Hostage* is an epitome: behind the whirl of song and dance and slapstick, national, religious, moral and political prejudices are mocked. Any critical analysis of *An Giall* must disclose a related theme: the dehumanising effect of strict political prejudices or ideologies. The critic tries to write a prose correlative of what the playwright has done, but there is an essential difference between the rational method of the critic and the imaginative method of the playwright. The playwright feels his way through the medium of character; to pre-impose his own rational views would tend to deprive the play of that tension which is its essential dramatic quality. The critic works in the opposite way, beginning with conclusions and working backwards. To begin with, Joan Littlewood had no first-hand knowledge of the original play, or even a direct translation; her ideas were based on descriptive commentary and her subsequent work on the play was, of necessity, based on criticism. The Theatre Workshop knew that *An Giall* condemned political prejudice; it was up to them to communicate this to their audiences. A London (or a New York) audience could not be expected to be as interested in the IRA as a Dublin audience; the theme of prejudice must therefore be related to world politics, to the sufferings of blacks, homosexuals, and developing nations under the threat of outworn systems and nuclear bombs. Miss Littlewood's contribution was a prodigious theatrical skill. It is doubtful if there ever was a full script and so it was necessary to flesh out the ideas they had, to emend what text they had and to ask Behan for what they felt was required. In the adaptation of what was known of *An Giall*, Miss Littlewood showed an uncanny ability to produce a performance which filled the theatre with delighted audiences and which elicited from critics the social responses which were the objectives of the Workshop. It is not suggested here that the existing text of *The Hostage* is not the work of Behan, but that the principles of the play are those of Miss Littlewood rather than those of the author of *An Giall*. Behan became part of the team, writing at times to order and accepting changes for which he was not responsible. *An Giall* is dramatic; *The Hostage* uses all the resources of the theatre to communicate fixed ideas and is, in that sense, theatrical.

If, as Behan claimed, Miss Littlewood suited his requirements exactly, the satisfaction was almost certainly mutual. Behan could be presented as one who had suffered because of his social background; his rise from slum-poverty to international repute via political imprisonment licensed him to comment on the human condition, while his left-wing leanings enabled him to fit in with the Workshop. But, perhaps even more important was the fact that Behan was a brilliantly theatrical person himself, a wit, raconteur and entertainer. He frequently appeared in the theatre during the run of *The Hostage*, adding to the general good spirits by joking with the actors and singing songs. He had a genius for self-advertisement and publicity and loved to be the centre of attraction among a crowd of happy people. The showman in him would have been very much at home in the Theatre Workshop, delighted to supply songs, snippets and jokes as they were required, happy to accept the advice of a producer who could almost guarantee success, applause, fame and money.

Fortunately or unfortunately, Behan was more than a show-man. More than a desire for applause had gone into his Irish poetry, *The Quare Fellow* and *Borstal Boy*; the decision to write *An Giall* is almost inexplicable unless one takes account of his quieter ambitions and of his desire, as a writer, to write better books and better plays. Even as he relished the rewards of his previous work, he realised that being a celebrity made it more difficult for him to progress as a writer. His brother Brian heard him cursing Joan Littlewood: 'I was surprised and I looked at him closely. He looked suddenly as if he knew he had been "taken for a ride", that he had been adopted as a broth of a boy, that they had played a three card trick on him. I think he sud-denly had a moment of insight which was gone as soon as the next joke or drink came round.'[17] It was unfair of Behan to blame Joan Littlewood for the dilemma in which he found himself, almost as unfair of his brother to accuse 'them'. Nobody had forced Behan to do anything. It is true that the temptations offered by the media, publishers and producers were almost irresistible for one who had always longed for praise and success, but the failure to resist them was his alone. If he had written nothing other than *Borstal Boy* he would still have learned enough about the hard grind of composition to suspect that it needed more than a few hoary jokes and instant-songs to make a play.[18]

7

Last Years 1958-1964

The story of Behan's last years has been told by two people who were close to him at the time and it is not the kind of story which invites retelling.[1] This brief conclusion is not concerned with all the details of his decline and fall, merely with his efforts to survive as a writer.

In 1958 everything seemed to go right for him. *An Giall* was a success, *The Hostage* a triumph. With the publication of *Borstal Boy* he could feel that the years of struggle were being amply rewarded: not only was he commercially successful, but he had also received critical acclaim. His extravagant personality and his ready wit made him a favourite with media-men who passed on his opinions to the world. And everything suggested that his success would increase rather than diminish: people clamoured for interviews, for the film rights of *The Quare Fellow*, the paperback rights of *Borstal Boy*, for permission to stage *The Hostage* in France and Germany. There were some disappointments—*The Quare Fellow* did not go down too well in New York and was slated in Berlin—but not enough to dent his prestige. In 1959 *The Hostage* was chosen to represent Britain at the Théâtre des Nations Festival in Paris and afterwards moved to the West End of London where it took on a new lease of life.

It was not only as an author that he made the news. In March 1959 he was charged with being drunk and disorderly in a small town outside Dublin. The case was widely publicised, not only because Behan was the defendant but also because he insisted that it be heard in Irish. During the following month he celebrated the Paris production of *The Hostage* by going on an alcoholic rampage which involved him in several fights. Very shortly afterwards, he released all his anti-social tendencies during several weeks of hard drinking in London.

Behan had grown up among people who immediately thought of celebration in terms of alcohol and he himself had been drinking for as long as he could remember. To a certain extent his sprees were predictable but only to a certain extent. Earlier on, while working as a journalist, he had realised that his drinking was not always based on a desire to celebrate but was often a means of escape. In 1956 his toasting of *The Quare Fellow* had landed him in hospital where he had learned that he was a diabetic and that unless he controlled his diet he risked serious injury to his system. Even while lamenting his loss of physical fitness and handsome features, he had continued to drink excessively.

His first alcoholic seizure coincided with the move of *The Hostage* to the West End in the summer of 1959. He remained in hospital only long enough to recover sufficient energy for a trip to London and a three-day binge which amazed all who witnessed it. He disrupted a performance of his own play and generally raised hell, emerged from a diabetic coma to wander into a punch-up and find himself in a cell. Back in Dublin, he wrote a newspaper article in which he admitted to being an alcoholic who was convinced he could cure himself. Behind the public optimism he was depressed by his inability to control his drinking. In January 1960, Rae Jeffs arrived in Dublin to conduct a literary experiment: she would tape-record Behan's thoughts on Ireland and he would later edit the transcripts into a book which he had contracted to supply. Despite one or two lapses into drunkenness, he returned to something like his old self and worked hard on the tapes. He began a new play called *Richard's Cork Leg* but soon afterwards he suffered another breakdown in London. This seemed to shock him into sense: he entered a special hospital and, though he left prematurely, he continued to improve. Even though lionised during a visit to the United States, he remained remarkably temperate and came home to get on with his writing. Joan Littlewood arrived in Dublin to discuss *Richard's Cork Leg*: having read the draft she felt that it needed more work before they could talk of a production. Though he pretended non-chalance, his pride was hurt. He dashed off an Irish version and took it to Gael Linn, but they also demanded revision. The result was that he exploded and, in the words of Rae Jeffs, 'remained in varying degrees of intoxication until the day he died'.[2]

Any comprehensive analysis of this self-punitive series of

drinking bouts would have to include elements which are outside the scope of this study—the physiology of diabetes and alcoholism, the psychology of alienation. In previous accounts of Behan's inability to come to terms with fame, one aspect of the pattern has been insufficiently stressed: the parallel between the graphs of his masochistic decline and of his attitude to writing.

In January 1958 he sought to avoid the social pressures of Ireland and England by going to Ibiza, hoping to get back to habits of industry, to complete *An Giall* and to begin a new novel, *the catacombs*. The move was not really effective: he could not resist the holiday aura of the island and his health suffered. Both play and novel proved intractable, yet developed in radically different manners after his sojourn on Ibiza. *An Giall* and its later mutation, *The Hostage*, were to varying extents induced through the midwifery of managers and producers and were greeted with enthusiasm; *the catacombs*, more dependant on its own volition, remained a stillborn fragment of 12,000 words, a niggling witness of his failure to sustain the effort of *Borstal Boy*.

The fragment begins:

> There was a party to celebrate Deirdre's return from her abortion in Bristol. Ciaran, her brother, welcomed me, literally with open arms, when I entered the Catalonian Cabinet Room where the guests were assembled. Even her mother, Maria, the screwy old bitch, came over with a glass of whiskey in her hand and said,
> 'You're welcome, Brendan Behan.'[3]

The bulk of the piece is devoted to an account of Deirdre's family and of the party. The Bolivars are Hispano-Irish, importing Spanish wine and exporting Irish potatoes. After tangential tales of Hispano-Irish political relations, the reader learns that Mr and Mrs Bolivar finally parted when she 'dropped the Ibizenco Fish-weight on the head of the President of the Scottish Widows' Mutual Financial Trust.' Brendan Behan is a working-class writer engaged on his memoirs of a political sentence in England. After much singing and drinking, he sleeps with Deirdre—an action resented by her brother on class rather than on moral grounds. In the morning, armed with a ten-pound note sent by Mr Bolivar, he goes to the Market for a curing drink. The reader recognises the pub from the *Irish Press* sketches: Michael is still there, as is Mr Crippen. Behan produces his note and orders drinks.

'A blue one, be Jasus!' said Crippen. 'Now aren't you the great sport, though, Brendan Behan!'

There the fragment ends.

There is no knowing what Behan might have made of *the catacombs*, what direction it would have taken in later drafts, but it is difficult to be optimistic. There are some jokes, some interesting moments, but on the whole it is neither gripping nor particularly funny. The attempts to play around with literary conventions do not come off: '[The Fianna Fáil crowd] would always grant his Holiness censorship of immoral publications (such as the one I am writing now), but a tariff or a trading quota was, as my sincere colleague the late Anton Chekhov would say, a character out of a different opera.' As a character, Brendan Behan is not subjected to the critical distancing which seasoned the admiration for him in *Borstal Boy* and there is an element of unattractive vanity in the author's intrusions. It is not difficult to see why the fragment ends where it does. The writer must have felt, as the reader feels, that aimlessness and lack of creative energy had led him back into the comfort of an old haunt. By now Behan knew that the novel demanded the persistent industry that had gone into *Borstal Boy*. All he had was a preliminary draft of a possible opening. He was finding it hard to commit himself to the drudgery of composition. Had he been an unknown the choice would have been simple—work or quit—but his perception had been distorted by events.

He had spent years on *The Quare Fellow* before seeing it staged. It had done well in Dublin and London but had been roughly handled by critics in New York and Berlin. On the other hand, he had barely managed to put the script of *An Giall* together in time, but it had been a success. During the final stages of the production of *The Hostage* he had more or less ceded control of the play to the producer and yet this had won him an international reputation. He could be forgiven for wondering if the success of the outcome was in inverse proportion to the effort. It was an attractive possibility but not one to convince him in his quieter moments. His first serious breakdown came with the promotion of *The Hostage* to the West End. His notorious disruption of the play and his subsequent self-obliteration in alcohol make psychological sense if it is assumed that part of him rejected what had happened to *An Giall*. He often announced that success was killing him. Typically, it was a shrewd observation disguised in grisly humour. People took it to mean that the income from his works was enough to subsidise a life of hedonism which was beyond his physical capacity, but he knew that there was much more to it. The easy success of *The Hostage* constituted a temptation as attractive and as lethal as alcohol which was destroying his ability to return to the craft of writing. Fears for his future as a writer disturbed him and such was his market value that even his failure to control himself was newsworthy and, inasmuch as he longed for the limelight, was itself a kind of success. His major breakdowns almost always followed some insight into this vicious circle, such as when he contrasted the triumphal march of *The Hostage* with the paralysis of *the catacombs*.

The same pattern is evident in his second and third breakdowns. He welcomed Rae Jeffs' tape-recorder in January 1960 not as a substitute for writing but as a means of returning to it. 'If the Mycenaean poets could do it, then so can I. I do not set myself up as an authority on these matters, but if Homer is to be believed, the Greeks wrote their books by improvising them in talk.'[4] His initial energy slackened as he tired of the project: he had undertaken to produce such a book merely to make money and knew that, at best, he was marking time.[5] He wanted to get back to his typewriter and to the new play, *Richard's Cork Leg*. Having worked on it for less than a month, he bolted to London and drank himself into a coma. Many reasons have been given for this suicidal binge but it seems most likely that it was a result of his failure to get his play moving, just as his previous collapse had taken place because of a similar experience with the *catacombs*.

He made an astonishing recovery and returned to Dublin and the play. While admitting that 'the sixty-four pages of manuscript were no more than notes for it', he instructed Rae Jeffs to look after the advance publicity for the play. She pointed out that the story was identical with that of *the catacombs*; Behan retorted that he 'could see no harm in this as the titles were quite different'.[6] In December 1960 he offered it to those who had launched *An Giall* and *The Hostage* but they turned it down. It must have dawned on him that they would only reject a new Behan play if it was absolutely unworkable. Unable to understand why this was so, unwilling to face the possibility that he was written-out, a failure, perhaps even a fraud, he drank himself into his third breakdown and never again regained his faith in himself as a writer.

During the remaining three years he tried to revive the past rather than attempt to shape a future. He returned to America, scene of his most recent triumph, but things had changed. He was a haunted man, always on the move, in and out of hospitals. He came home to Ireland, not to the friends he had made when famous, but to those he had known before all that, especially his IRA comrades. He knew that he was dying and made them promise that he would be given an IRA funeral.[7] He was no longer the author of *Borstal Boy* and *An Giall*. The desire for a republican funeral was his ultimate rejection of everything associated with the literary success which he knew had killed him. He never wrote anything else. He recorded *Confessions of an Irish Rebel* and *Brendan Behan's New York* in 1963, more out of the necessity to honour contracts than from any creative drive. In 1963 a selection of his *Irish Press* sketches was revived as *Hold Your Hour and Have Another*; a year later came *The Scarperer* in book form.

Richard's Cork Leg had been the turning-point. As in the case of *the catacombs*, it is unfair to treat it as a finished work. A happier Behan would have worked on it, gradually discovering his theme and structure. At the time, he felt otherwise. For all his talk about music hall and the problems of the contemporary playwright, he knew little of dramatic theory and cared less, preferring to leave such speculations to the critics.[8] *The Hostage* had succeeded despite the general feeling that 'its line of action is not vital and its scenes, with a few obvious exceptions, are almost interchangeable';[9] why should he bother with plot or structure? It was the atmosphere and energy of the play which had won people over; surely the same spirit in a different form would conquer them again? He had done it all before, almost casually; how could he possibly fail now if he put his mind to it? Choose a setting which is visually striking, bring on a few colourful characters, introduce sex, religion and politics, and baste well with song-and-dance, stand-up jokes, slapstick business and some references to himself.

Richard's Cork Leg was obviously written to such a formula. As a piece of pure entertainment its major fault is that it is no longer new.[10] Various lumps of raw material were thrown into the cauldron and spoiled. The story of Honor Bright, a prostitute with whose ugly murder a police officer and a doctor were charged and whose grave is a place of annual pilgrimage for the united prostitutes of disunited Ireland, had unlimited potential in the hands of the man who had written *The Quare Fellow*. The principal male character, The Leper Cronin, is a witty critic of left, right and centre, cheerful despite his disenchantment with all that organised society had to offer, a selfish philanthropist. It is tantalising to wonder what the author of *Borstal Boy* would have made of him if Cronin were given *his* novel or *his* play. But the ore of the draft, which would have been refined in the process of rewriting, is wasted. The sparkle of the two whores is dulled by some appallingly decrepit jokes and the Honor Bright motif is allowed to fizzle out. Cronin competes for our attention with a black aristocrat who plans to transform the Irish graveyard into another Forest Lawn, and with a shortsighted dramatist who neglects him time after time in search of cheap laughs. The title of the play is apt even though it is totally irrelevant to the action. The story goes that Joyce, having had a play rejected as too gloomy, remarked that he might have fared better had he given Richard, one of the characters, a cork leg. Unlike Joyce, Behan was willing to 'jolly things up' to suit the public.[11]

There is little to be said in favour of the Irish version, *Lá Breá san Roilg* (A Fine Day in the Graveyard), which has all the faults and none of the virtues of the English. That Behan should have expected Gael Linn to welcome it showed how blurred his critical faculty had become. It reads like a translation of an earlier and cruder form of *Richard's Cork Leg* and is in one act.[12] Instead of the black Bonnie Prince Charlie who had some nominal business in the graveyard, there is the Aga Khan who has none. The whores have great difficulty with the Irish language and Cronin is not nearly as witty or as interesting. The jokes and slapstick are remarkably unfunny and the conclusion a weak echo of *The Hostage*. Cronin makes love to Deirdre on a tombstone as the lights go down; in the returning light an unknown skeleton arises from an unknown grave and joins the others in a dance. The skeleton may be that of Honor Bright but the music is the author's favourite tune, 'The Blackbird'.[13]

Notes

1. TRADITION AND THE INDIVIDUAL TALENT
(pp. 1–24)

1. Ulick O'Connor, *Brendan Behan* (London 1970), 13.
2. Seamus de Burca, *The Soldier's Song* (Dublin 1957), 13–28.
3. O'Connor, 13.
4. Brendan Behan, *Borstal Boy*, Corgi edition (London 1964), 80. Future references to *BB*.
5. See O'Connor, 14.
6. *BB*, 80.
7. See Seamus de Burca, *Brendan Behan*, Proscenium Chapbooks, I (Delaware 1971), 11–13; and Brendan Behan, *Confessions of an Irish Rebel*, Arrow edition (London 1967), 254f. Future references to latter as *CIR*.
8. O'Connor, 16f.
9. Brendan Behan, *Hold Your Hour and Have Another* (London 1963), 85f. Future references to *HHHA*.
10. O'Connor, 20.
11. O'Connor, 30.
12. O'Connor, 23.
13. *Irish Democrat* (Dublin), 6 November 1937.
14. *CIR*, 217.
15. Brendan Behan, *Brendan Behan's Island* (London 1962), 26. Future references to *BBI*.
16. See de Burca, *Brendan Behan*, 19, and Behan's note on the jacket of de Burca's *The Soldier's Song*.
17. See, for example, Seamus G. O'Kelly, 'I Knew the Real Brendan Behan', *The Irish Digest* (June 1964), 67. Ulick O'Connor's claim (p. 31) that Behan contributed to *The United Irishman* is impossible: the paper did not exist at the time and only re-emerged as an IRA publication in 1948. It is likely that Behan wrote more than I have been able to establish: there is no doubt that he wrote several pieces on the Spanish Civil War which appeared over the signature *Young Dublin Worker*, but although I have spoken to

people who remember them, I have been unable to locate them. See Cathal Goulding's remark in Beatrice Behan, *My Life with Brendan* (London 1973), 73.

18. See, for example, his 'Easter Day' in the *United Irishman*, May 1948, and the following verses transcribed from the original manuscript by kind permission of its owner, Mr Sean Nolan.

'Twill pass—this time of rotting sorrow,
Of toiling slaves and crushing woe,
This night's tears will pass into the morrow,
As night into the morning's glow.

You're doomed, dead time of prostitutes and princes
Of regal splendour and of hungry pain
Of overlord and craven bondman
Of victim's loss and pompous victor's gain.

And none shall mourn, nor in thy funeral's pass
Shall drop a tear or aid thee in death's strife
But turning to the new day from thy carcass,
With outstretched arms shall cheer the birth of Life.

Sean Nolan also remembers verses by Behan on an Irish boy who died in the Korean War and on a child from Kimmage who was drowned.

19. De Burca, *Brendan Behan*, 14.

2. FREELANCE 1941–1956 (pp. 25–45)

1. See J. Bowyer Bell, *The Secret Army* (London 1970), chapter 11.
2. See O'Connor, 62–8, and *The World of Brendan Behan*, edited by Sean McCann (London 1965), 50f.
3. *CIR*, 31.
4. Seán Ó Briain, 'I Knew Brendan Behan', *The Kerryman*, 23 May 1964.
5. Ó Briain, 'I Knew Brendan Behan'.
6. See 82f. below.
7. See O'Connor, 78. The manuscript of *The Execution* is in the library of University College, Cork.
8. Ó Briain, 'I Knew Brendan Behan'.
9. *CIR*, 80.
10. The view expressed by O'Connor, p. 109, is supported by those who knew Behan at the time.
11. I am indebted to Maitiú Ó Néill for this information.
12. See 67 below.

13. The prisoner's account is given by O'Connor, 128f.
14. Sindbad Vail, quoted by O'Connor, 141.
15. Letter from Behan to Vail, quoted by O'Connor, 143.
16. See O'Connor, 148.
17. McCann, 181.
18. McCann, 186. The articles appeared in *Comhar* in October, November, December, January, March and April 1952/53.
19. See introduction by Mícheál Ó hAodha to Brendan Behan, *Moving Out and A Garden Party*, edited by Robert Hogan (California 1967).
20. The story was broadcast on Radio Éireann and first appeared in *The Standard*, Easter 1953, p.5.
21. *CIR*, 240. The 'pornography' referred to is almost certainly *After the Wake*.
22. Brendan Behan, *The Scarperer* (New York 1964), 124.
23. *The Scarperer*, 72.
24. *HHHA*, 32.
25. *HHHA*, 61f.
26. *HHHA*, 90f.

3. BEHAN'S IRISH POETRY (pp. 46–61)
(*Translations from Irish are my own.*)
1. Máirtín Ó Cadhain, *As an nGéibheann* (Dublin 1973), 201.
2. There is no collection of Behan's verse. Nine of the poems first published in *Comhar* were reprinted in the April 1964 number. 'The Return of McCaughey' was omitted, possibly because it was originally printed over the initial B. 'Grafton Street' appeared in *Feasta*, August 1949, and 'Loneliness' in *Envoy*, January 1950.
3. Letter to *Irish Democrat*, 6 November 1937.
4. For example, Máirtín Ó Cadhain wrote at the time (p. 142): '. . . being imprisoned here has changed me in many ways. I am sure of myself and able to relate my reading to my life as never before.'
5. See Chapters 4 and 5 below.
6. Ó Cadhain, 151.
7. Seán Ó Tuama (ed.), *Nuabhéarsáíocht* (Dublin 1950), 9f.
8. See O'Connor, 83, and Chapter 4, below.
9. The 'Pádraic' addressed in the opening line of the poem is puzzling until it is recognised that Behan based the first quatrain on an earlier poem by Liam Dall Ó hIfearnáin (1720–1803) entitled *A Phádraig na nÁrann*. See R. Ó Foghludha, *Ar bruach na Coille Muaire* (Dublin 1939), 58f.

10. Irish does not lend itself to full-rime. The *ambrán* (song) is based on a pattern of vowel-rime which includes both end-line and mid-line consonance.
11. See *CIR*, 121, and Rae Jeffs, *Brendan Behan : Man and Showman* (London 1966), 33.
12. *BBI* 70. Behan is mistaken (?) when he writes that he was serving fourteen years at the time.
13. Valentine Iremonger's translations of the Blaskets, Joyce and Wilde poems are included in *Brendan Behan's Island*.
14. See *Borstal Boy*, 319. Ó Briain also used his time in Mountjoy to study the poetry of Dáibhí Ó Bruadair, another master of rhetorical satire.
15. See *BB*, 136 and 238.
16. Cf. *The Black Tower* by Yeats.

4. THE QUARE FELLOW (pp. 62–80)

1. *CIR*, 254.
2. See Chapter 2 above.
3. De Burca, *Brendan Behan*, 19f.
4. O'Connor, 74.
5. O'Connor, 75.
6. Behan to Bob Bradshaw, quoted by O'Connor, 77f.
7. Quoted by O'Connor, 75. In an interesting letter to Seamus de Burca from Arbour Hill Detention Barracks, dated 16 August 1943, Behan wrote that he detected the influence of Synge—'an odd flush of Synge'—in the language of *The Landlady*. He quoted a convincing example which included : 'For a darin' demon is the divil's darlin', an' it's the brave glimmer man 'd trust himself to yer likes.' The letter is quoted in full in the *Irish Press*, 11 March 1976.
8. Quoted by O'Connor, 83. Although O'Connor does not say so, the correspondence seems to have been originally in Irish.
9. O'Connor, 81.
10. See Chapter 2 above.
11. *CIR*, 56.
12. When his publisher was unsure as to the suitability of the title *Borstal Boy*, Behan suggested *This Young Neck* as an alternative. See *Jeffs*, 41.
13. O'Kelly, 69f.
14. See *CIR*, 239f.; de Burca, Brendan Behan, 24; and Mícheál Ó hAodha's introduction to *Moving Out and A Garden Party*, 4f.
15. The story of the Pike production is told in Alan Simpson, *Beckett and Behan and a Theatre in Dublin* (London 1962).

16. Figures in brackets refer to pages in first edition of *The Quare Fellow* (London 1956).
17. Raymond J. Porter, *Brendan Behan* (New York 1973), 20.
18. See, for example, Ted E. Boyle, *Brendan Behan* (New York 1969), 67.
19. The character of Regan was modified for the London production. See O'Connor, 186–8.
20. See, for example, Judith Crist quoted by Boyle, 70, and *Die Welt* quoted by O'Connor, 219f.

5. BORSTAL BOY (pp. 81–116)

1. Quoted by O'Connor, 77f.
2. See Chapter 2 above.
3. See 24 above.
4. Twelve pages, entitled *The Courteous Borstal*, now in the Morris Library, Southern Illinois University. This and other Behan autographs in the Morris Library are described by Corey Phelps, 'Borstal Revisited', *ICarbS*, 11/1 (1975), 39–60. The dating is tentative, based on Behan's difficulties in expressing his attitude towards Borstal.
5. *The Courteous Borstal* is almost illegible because of all the crossing out and correction. I have made no effort to reproduce the manuscript in all its chaos, but have tried to strike a balance between Behan's final version and the interesting sections he deleted. On the first page of the manuscript there are calculations as to the number of words in it, which suggests that Behan had publication in mind.
6. See 66f. above.
7. See Chapter 1, note 11.
8. Jeffs, 33.
9. See 51f. above.
10. *Comhar*, January 1953, 9f.
11. *CIR*, 232.
12. Quoted by O'Connor, 142, 147.
13. See Phelps, 'Borstal Revisited'.
14. Phelps, 47–56; and Boyle, 103–5.
15. Neither Phelps nor Boyle distinguishes between the creative objectives of the typescript and the novel.
16. No IRA man would dream of associating the heroically staunch Emmet with de Valera the betrayer of the Republic.
17. See 106 below.
18. *BB*, 278.
19. *BB*, 303.

20. McCann, 63. The extracts, which were published in *The People,* October-November 1958, to coincide with the publication of *Borstal Boy,* had appeared previously in the Irish edition of the *Sunday Dispatch,* September-October 1956; they read like articles specially prepared for newspaper serialisation rather than like extracts from a novel. Entitled *Bridewell Revisited,* an account of the Borstal Nativity Play was published in the *New Statesman,* 8 December 1956. 'Christmas Day in Walton Jail', which differs only slightly from pp. 111–22 of the novel, appeared in *Irish Writing,* 35 (1957).

21. Episodes in the first two sections normally fulfilled two functions, describing the physical confinement and pointing to some psychological development in the prisoner; in the final section much is included that is simply descriptive. There is a certain amount of repetition—of Raftery's poem on spring, of the song called 'The Sea Around Us' (albeit on request) and of the crack about the Behan land being in window-boxes. An example of the most damaging kind of repetition is the fight with Perry. As a description of a fight it is not bad but it fails miserably to live up to the standard set by the assault on James in Walton Jail and it tells the reader nothing new about Behan.

22. Jeffs, 21.

23. Jeffs, 33.

24. One has only to compare the texture of *Borstal Boy* with that of the dictated *Confessions of an Irish Rebel.*

25. Figures in brackets refer to pages in *Borstal Boy,* Corgi edition (London 1964).

26. James Joyce, *A Portrait of the Artist as a Young Man,* Penguin Modern Classics edition (London 1972), 203.

6. AN GIALL AND THE HOSTAGE (pp. 117–134)

1. See, for example, O'Connor, 191.

2. Porter, 31.

3. The play is most readily available in *Brendan Behan's Island.*

4. BBI, 110.

5. McCann, 186f.

6. O'Connor, 192.

7. Quoted by O'Connor, 193.

8. De Burca, *Brendan Behan,* 30.

9. Figures in brackets refer to pages in *An Giall* (An Chomhairle Náisiúnta Drámaíochta, Dublin, n.d.). The translations are my own.

10. See 49f. above.

11. For the remainder of this chapter, figures in brackets refer to pages in *The Hostage*, 3rd edition, revised (London 1962).
12. See O'Connor, 196f.
13. See O'Connor, 186–8.
14. *BBI*, 17.
15. Wolf Mankovitz, quoted by O'Connor, 196.
16. Quoted by O'Connor, 199 and 228.
17. Quoted by O'Connor, 208.
18. Apart from one or two songs, there is little verbal comedy in the play.

7. LAST YEARS 1958–1964 (pp. 135–142)
1. Beatrice Behan and Rae Jeffs.
2. Jeffs, 149.
3. I am grateful to Beatrice Behan who allowed me to examine a copy of the fragment.
4. Jeffs, 114.
5. *Brendan Behan's Island*, prepared for publication by Rae Jeffs and including a good deal of earlier material, is a pleasant book and was well received. Behan never really accepted it as his own and was loth to inscribe copies for his friends.
6. Jeffs, 142f.
7. Dominic Behan, *My Brother Brendan* (London 1965), 153.
8. See, for example, Jeffs, 33.
9. McCann, 124.
10. It was 'finished' and produced by Alan Simpson.
11. Jeffs, 143.
12. I am indebted to Seán Ó Briain for a copy of *Lá Breá san Roilg*. It is either a transcript of a tape or a professional copy of a difficult typescript. O'Connor's account of its origins (p. 270) is more likely than Jeff's (p. 148), although there is the impression that while writing *Lá Breá san Roilg* Behan either had some preliminary notes in English or was, perhaps, thinking in English—in places it reads like a translation. Somebody has read over the typescript, querying obscurities and crossing out inferior passages. Some indication of the level may be gained from a rejected episode. Cronin has boasted that he can recognise any brand of whiskey by taste. One of the whores tests him by offering him samples of Jameson, Haig and her own urine.
13. After the play, the voice of Behan (who does not appear in the play) is heard : he blesses the play, salutes the audience and sings a song which he claims was too obscene to be included in the play.

SELECT BIBLIOGRAPHY

(I) BOOKS BY BRENDAN BEHAN
An Giall, Dublin n.d.
Borstal Boy, London 1958.
Brendan Behan's Island, London 1962.
Brendan Behan's New York, London 1964.
Confessions of an Irish Rebel, London 1965.
Hold Your Hour and Have Another, London 1963.
Moving Out and *A Garden Party*, edited by Robert Hogan, California 1967.
Richard's Cork Leg, introduced, edited and with additional material by Alan Simpson, London 1973.
The Hostage, London 1958.
The Quare Fellow, London 1956.
The Scarperer, New York 1964.

(II) BOOKS BY OTHER AUTHORS
Behan, Beatrice, *My Life with Brendan*, London 1973.
Behan, Brian, *With Breast Expanded*, London 1964.
Behan, Dominic, *My Brother Brendan*, London 1965.
Bell, J. Bowyer, *The Secret Army*, London 1970.
Boyle, Ted E., *Brendan Behan*, New York 1969.
Burca, Seamus de, *Brendan Behan*, Delaware 1971.
Burca, Seamus de, *The Soldier's Song*, Dublin 1957.
Clarke, Thomas J., *Glimpses of an Irish Felon's Prison Life*, Dublin 1922.
Davitt, Michael, *Leaves from a Prison Diary*, London 1885.
Devoy, John, *Recollections of an Irish Rebel*, New York 1929.
Jeffs, Rae, *Brendan Behan: Man and Showman*, London 1966.
McCann, Sean, ed., *The World of Brendan Behan*, London 1965.
Merriman, Brian, *Cúirt an Mheán Óiche*, edited by Dáithí Ó hUaithne, Dublin 1968.
Mitchel, John, *Jail Journal*, Dublin 1854.
Ó Cadhain, Máirtín, *As an nGéibheann*, Dublin 1973.
O'Connor, Ulick, *Brendan Behan*, London 1970.
Ó hAodha, Mícheál, *Theatre in Ireland*, Oxford 1974.
Ó Tuama, Seán, *Nuabhéarsaíocht*, Dublin 1950.
Porter, Raymond J., *Brendan Behan*, New York 1973.
Ryan, John, *Remembering How We Stood*, Dublin 1975.

Simpson, Alan, *Beckett and Behan and a Theatre in Dublin*, London 1962.

Sullivan, T.D., A.M., and D.B., *Speeches from the Dock*, Dublin n.d.

Tone, Theobald Wolfe, *The Autobiography*, abridged and edited by Sean O'Faolain, London 1937.

Index